WITHDRAWN

Wayne E. Rickerson

GETTING YOUR FAMILY TOGETHER

PB155 20

A Guidebook to Christian Parenting

A Division of G/L Publications FAMILY LIFE LIBRARY
Glendale, California, U.S.A. REGAL BOOKS

66952

Other good Regal reading:
Good Times for Your Family
    by Wayne E. Rickerson
You Can't Begin Too Soon
    by Wesley Haystead
How to Succeed in Family Living
    by Clyde M. Narramore
The Celebration Book
    by Georgiana Walker
Measure of a Family
    by Gene A. Getz
You Can Have a Happier Family
    by Norm Wakefield

Scripture quotations in this publication, unless otherwise
indicated, are from the *Authorized King James
Version*. Other versions quoted are:
NASB, New American Standard Bible. © The Lockman
Foundation 1960, 1962, 1963, 1968, 1971. Used by permission.
Phillips, THE NEW TESTAMENT IN MODERN ENGLISH, Revised
Edition, J.B. Phillips, Translator. © J.B. Phillips 1958,
1960, 1972. Used by permission of Macmillan Publishing Co., Inc.
RSV, From *Revised Standard Version* of the Bible, copyrighted 1946
and 1952 by the Division of Christian Education of the NCCC,
U.S.A., and used by permission.
TLB, From *The Living Bible,* Copyright © 1971 by Tyndale House
Publishers, Wheaton, Illinois. Used by permission.

Second Printing, 1978

Published by Regal Books Division, G/L Publications
Glendale, California 91209. Printed in U.S.A.

Library of Congress Catalog Card No. 77-78848
ISBN 0-8307-0426-4

Contents

Life with the Super Family

I would like you to meet the Super family. Mr. Super, a successful engineer, is active in community affairs, serves on the school board, is a Little League coach, loves to hunt and fish, teaches the junior boys' Sunday School class and is a deacon in charge of building and grounds.

His wife, Mrs. Super, is equally as interesting and energetic. She makes sure the children arrive on time at all their sports events and enrichment activities, is the leader of a women's Bible study group, serves as vice-president of the PTA, and is one of the sponsors of the Sunday night junior high youth group.

The Supers have two charming children. Joan Super, age 9, does well in school, is a good little pianist, takes tumbling and art lessons each week, is a member of the

Girl Scouts, and is active in the church junior youth group.

Her brother Mike, age 13, is quite an athlete. In fact it looks as if he will letter in football, basketball and track this year, which makes Mr. Super tremendously proud of his son. But Mike has more going than just sports. He is an honor student, president of the church youth group, and will become an Eagle Scout sometime this year.

Now let's take a look at the Super family's schedule for one day, Wednesday for example. Breakfast is staggered (in more ways than one) because Mr. Super leaves early for his 45-minute drive to work and Mike leaves for school one half hour before Joan.

Wednesday is one of Mrs. Super's relatively easy days. Other than a few calls for the PTA, study for her women's Bible study class, washing, ironing, cleaning, and cooking, she has little to do until it is time to take Joan to her piano lesson at 3:00.

Wednesday dinner at the Supers' is a kind of gulp-as-you-gallop affair because they must leave by 6:45 for Family Night at the church. Mrs. Super usually puts out sandwiches and chips and dip because schedules are so varied. Joan is hungry at 5:30, Mike arrives home famished at 6:00 after football practice and Mr. Super looks for a bite at about 6:15 after a hard day's work.

At 6:45 everyone piles into the car and heads for church. The Supers arrive at one minute to 7:00, jump out of the car and head for their classes. "What elective are you going to take this quarter, dear?" asks Mr. Super. "I guess I'll take the one on family unity taught by the Pastor," answers Mrs. Super. "It looks really good. See you later."

Family Night is over and the Supers are in bed. We

watch as the last light is turned out, but we hear no "Good night, Joan," "Good night, Mike," "Good night, Dad," "Good night, Mom." The Supers are too tired for such things. After all, it's not easy being a Super family!

The Supers Are Not Alone

Nor is it easy to get *any* family together in our society. We all really sympathize with the plight of the Super family, for we see ourselves facing, in varying degrees, the same types of problems. None of us, no matter how strong his feelings for the family may be, is immune to the pressures modern society puts on us. The pace of life is incredibly fast, and family togetherness is given very low priority.

But as Christian parents who want our children to be committed to Christ and to be successful as human beings, it is essential that we fight for our family life.

Just how important is it for families to do things together? Very important, according to the *Report to the President, White House Conference on Children.* "A child learns, he becomes human, primarily through participation in a challenging activity with those he loves and admires . . . it is in work and play with children, in games, in projects, in shared responsibilities with parents, adults, and other children that the child develops the skills, motives, and qualities of character that enable him to live a life that is gratifying both to himself and those around him."[1]

The report goes on to say that because of the alarming decline in the amount of time adults are spending with children, we are experiencing "a breakdown in the process of making human beings human."[2]

Similar facts have been discovered by Urie Bronfenbrenner, Professor of Human Development and Family Studies at Cornell University. "It is noteworthy that of all the countries in which my colleagues and I are working, now numbering half a dozen both in the West and the East, the only one which exceeds the U.S. in the willingness of children to engage in antisocial behavior is the nation closest to us in our Anglo-Saxon traditions of individualism. That country is England . . . England is also the only country in our sample which showed a level of parental involvement lower than our own, with both parents especially fathers, showing less affection, offering less companionship and intervening less frequently in the lives of their children."[3]

The Biblical Pattern

As Christian parents we cannot afford such breakdowns in relationships with our children. God has placed in our hands unique human beings. He has asked us to cultivate in them Christian character and commitment. In order to do this we need to create a family atmosphere in which strong relationships can be built. Such relationships are the crucial factor in transmitting values.

We have a classic example of this style of family living in the Old Testament. The early Hebrew family was noted for its solidarity. This family unity developed quite naturally as the very nature of that society placed children and parents in close contact with one another. Almost all activities centered around the home. The Hebrew home was the primary educational, recreational and social center for the children. As a result, parents spent time with their children—teaching, communicating. This interaction helped produce the kind of family unity that made it possible to pass on values from parents to children, from generation to generation (see Ps. 78:4).

Several thousand years have not changed the basic principle that family relationships develop in homes where families spend time together, playing, listening, communicating, and sharing God's Word.

How can a husband love his wife as Christ loved the Church, giving Himself up for it (see Eph. 5:25), if he is going in so many directions that he does not have time to sense her needs? Or how can a wife "reverence" her husband (see Eph. 5:33) if her mind is focused on a dozen other things, no matter how noble they might be?

How can a father stimulate the faith and courage and give instruction (see 1 Thess. 2:11, *Phillips*) to each child if he is rarely home? How can his children possibly copy him if he vanishes before their eyes in a blur of activity? Is it possible for a father to avoid provoking his children (see Eph. 6:4) when he disciplines and teaches them if he has not already developed a close personal relationship with them?

Where will children learn the Christian values of love, respect, sensitivity, trust, manners, courage and communication, if the family is not together enough to live them out at home?

It is obvious that God, the master builder of homes (see Ps. 127) wants His carpenters, Christian parents, to put in a full shift using the correct tools, including His Word. If we don't, there is a good chance our homes will not stand the test of the stormy weather of family living which is a normal part of life.

Lessons from Experience

Unfortunately, many Christian parents find out the hard way that it takes time together to build Christian families. I was recently reminded of this when I asked a friend about the sons of a mutual acquaintance of ours. I fully expected the answer she gave, for this man, a noted Christian leader, spent little time with his family over the years. "The boys are really in bad shape spiritually," she said. "They couldn't care less about God. They are very bitter about a father who had time for God and everyone else, but none for them."

There are other Christian parents who take the time to build strong families. As president of a Bible college alumni association I had the privilege of awarding a scholarship to an outstanding high school senior. I asked the girl who received the scholarship what effect her family life had on her Christian commitment and academic achievement.

"Oh, I could go on forever about that," she bubbled. "Our family really communicated. You see, we always had family times right after supper. This was a session when we could talk about problems, or read Scripture or other good books. Often it was just informal sharing. Of course, our communication was not limited to family times. All of us kids felt that we could go to Mom or Dad any time and they would listen to us. We did not see them as being perfect but as people who had problems like us."

As this enthusiastic girl paused for breath, I broke in with another question. "But what happened when you reached junior high and high school? Did you still appreciate family times?"

"More than ever," she replied. "Because we didn't have them as often they were more precious. Now that I'm in college it is really great to go home and have a family time."

This is not an isolated case. Children, even teenagers,

need and value family time. However, the children will not call the family together. It is our responsibility as parents to see that we have a balanced Christian family life—one that includes regular family time!

Footnotes

1. *Report to the President, White House Conference on Children* (Washington D.C.: U.S. Government Printing Office, 1971), p. 241.
2. *Report to the President*, p. 242.
3. Urie Bronfenbrenner, *Two Worlds of Childhood* (New York: Pocket Books, Inc., 1973), p. 116.

2

We *Can* Have Family Together Time

It is not easy to find family time. In fact it's a battle all the way—a continuing battle. A mother confronted me recently with this problem. "I see the need for family time," she said, "but what do you do about a schedule like ours? We're rarely together, but it seems like everything we do is important. Can you help us evaluate our schedules?"

If you have a similar question about your own family schedule then I suggest that you use the following plan to evaluate it.

Make Family Time a Priority

Family time must move to the top of the priority list. Yes, ahead of meetings, enrichment activities, sports, hobbies, TV, or whatever is keeping your family apart.

As Bruce Narramore says, "The foundation for moral and spiritual training is our own set of priorities. There come times for each of us when we need to reflect carefully on our style of living and ask ourselves some fundamental questions. For us as Christian parents, one of these questions should surely be, 'What are the most important things in life to me?' "[1]

My wife and I were faced with such questions a few years ago. At the age of 29 with two small children, we felt convicted by God that we should prepare for a full-time Christian vocation. Ahead of us lay three years of undergraduate work and two years of seminary, and after that the pressures of a church staff position. My father was a pastor and missionary so I was well aware of the family life pressures on those church vocations.

We evaluated our priorities, and God and family led the list. We decided that the family would always be our primary concern—before school, before church work, before making a living, second only to our personal relationships with God.

I can honestly say that it has worked. We have held the line for nine years and the result is a very "together" family. It has always taken real effort. In the earlier years of our schooling it meant that I had to study early in the morning, many times beginning at 3:00 A.M., until time for my first class. Family time was from noon until 2:00 P.M. I worked from 2:30 to 8:30 P.M.

When I graduated from seminary and accepted my first full-time staff position as a director of Christian education, we faced new problems. How do we protect our family life and still meet the expectations of the church? We communicated our deep feelings about family life to the church, refused to become over-scheduled and as a result were able to preserve an adequate amount of family time. The church appreciated our stand on the family and was most cooperative in allowing us to follow our convictions.

Each family has its own set of "impossible circumstances" that hinder it from having enough family time. However, an irrefutable fact of life is that we do the things we feel are most important. If the family is at the top of our list of priorities, we will be able to find family time.

Evaluate Your Family Time

Once you decide you want to have more family time, the next concern is to make a careful evaluation of your family schedule. It is impossible for me to tell you how many hours a week you should spend with your family. There are too many variables and there is great variety in the types of activities families enjoy together. But there is a quality, a spirit, that is common to all successful family life.

To help you analyze the time your family spends together, I have developed the following four-step process of evaluation:

Step 1: Peer

Peer into your family schedule by filling out Family Time Form 1[2] (at the end of this chapter). Indicate all family members who spend time together in any activity by placing the initial of each participant in that activity and the amount of time spent at it in a given day. If the whole family is together, write *W.F.* and the amount of time spent together.

Next analyze your family schedule by asking yourself the following questions:

1. Do we have enough time together?

2. Is one person spending too much time away from the rest of the family?

3. Do we have a time each day when the whole family is together?

4. Do we have times during the week when we share together in God's Word?

5. Do we spend the significant portions of at least three evenings a week together as a family?

6. Do we have an average of one meal a day together during the week?

7. Are we spending too much time watching TV? (You might want to add up actual TV viewing hours.)

8. How many activities does our family participate in each week that separate the family rather than unite it? If you can resolve your problems with Step 1, then eliminate Steps 2, 3 and 4. However if you still have snags in your family schedule, complete all four steps.

Step 2: Peek

This activity is designed to give each family member a chance to analyze his own schedule and then give the rest of the family an opportunity to peek.

Make a copy of Family Time Form 2 (at the end of this chapter) for each family member and have him fill it out, indicating, in the appropriate column, the time he spends away from the family. Next he should circle the activities he feels are most important. The last step is for each person to place a check mark beside the activities he feels he could possibly do without.

Now share your individual schedules with one another and discuss the following questions:

Do you feel that the amount of time you spend at

home is about right, not enough, or too much?

Which of your activities do you consider indispensable?

Which activities could you possibly do without?

Step 3: Peel

Are you ready to take out the knife and start the painful process of peeling off some activities to make room for family time? Based on the information you have gleaned from Steps 1 and 2, discuss the following questions and see what new family time slots you can create:

What individual activities do we need to drop to make room for family activities?

What meetings or activities does the family attend that could be dropped and the time put to better use by doing something together at home?

Can we adjust the family schedule so that one night a week can be Family Night (at home)?

Is there some time when the family generally watches TV that could be put to better use by doing some activity together?

Step 4: Plan

Here is a very crucial step in our quest for meaningful family time. *We must plan for things to happen!* Opening up more hours for the family to be together is not the complete answer. For this time to be used to its fullest potential we need to plan activities that will help the family communicate, share Scripture, have fun, and really enjoy one another's company.

Probably the biggest stumbling block to meaningful family time is our failure to plan for family activities. I know that is true in our family. It amazes me how time slips away—and how the things we talk about doing never happen because we fail to set dates and times.

My wife and I found that a simple monthly family planning calendar helps us plan specific things for our family to do together. Each week my wife and I sit down with the calendar as a part of our sharing time and write on it what we would like to do during the week and month. We write such things as Family Night, reading together, spiritual birthdays, devotional times (and who is responsible), family recreation, church activities and weekend outings.

Family Time Form 3 (at the end of this chapter) is a copy of the planning calendar we use. We suggest you either make monthly copies of this calendar or purchase a similar one from a stationery supply store. Take time each week to plan for family activities. Further on in this book you will find many ideas for activities that your family will enjoy doing together. In my book *Good Times for Your Family* there are listed 100 short devotional activities for the family.[3] The bibliography at the end of this chapter gives a list of other books and resources that will provide you with a storehouse of ideas.

Watch the local newspaper for things your family can do together. Many schools, libraries, and recreation centers offer family activities. Have a family "brainbust." You will be amazed at the number of ideas for family activities you will think of in just fifteen minutes. When you have gathered lots of ideas, choose some for each week, write them on the family planning calendar for future activities.

Marjorie Holmes really captured the spirit of what I have been trying to say in a prayer entitled "Let me raise my own children." This is certainly my prayer, and I hope you will make it yours as we venture together through the remaining chapters of this book:

"Lord, help me to remember that nobody else can raise my children—not neighbors or maids or baby-sitters. It can't be done by schools or even by churches, important as they are. Not by Scouts or Little Leagues, or Y's; not by doctors or counselors, by choir directors or dancing teachers or by the hundred and one other people to whom we entrust our offspring for so many hours. . . .

"The years of their growing up are so precious, Lord, and so fleeting. Don't let me duck the responsibility you have given me along with the children. Help us all to sort out our priorities and to drop any activities that separate this family instead of uniting it.

"Give me a firm new grip on the challenge of raising my children—and a proud new joy in it."[4]

Amen!!!

Footnotes

1. S. Bruce Narramore, *Ounce of Prevention: A Parents' Guide to Moral and Spiritual Growth in Children* (Grand Rapids: Zondervan Publishing House, 1973), p. 26.
2. Adapted from "Family Time Indicator" by Norm Wakefield, *You Can Have a Happier Family* (Glendale, Calif.; Regal Books, 1977), p. 70.
3. Wayne E. Rickerson, *Good Times for Your Family* (Glendale, Calif.: Regal Books, G/L Publications, 1976).
4. Marjorie Holmes, *Hold Me Up a Little Longer, Lord* (New York: Doubleday and Company, Inc., 1977).

FAMILY TIME FORM 1

Instructions: Place the initial of family members who spend time together in the specific activity identified, as well as the amount of time spent. (Use W.F. for whole family.)

Activity	S	M	T	W	T	F	S
Breakfast together							
Lunch together							
Supper together							
Read aloud							
Recreation							
• Camping							
• Home recreation							
• Away recreation							
Regular travel time together							
• To church, shopping, etc.							
Hobbies							
Designated family night							
Working around house or yard							
Other _____							

FAMILY TIME FORM 2

Instructions: List the activity and times you spend away from the family. Circle the activities that are of most importance to you. Put a check mark beside the activities you can possibly do without.

	Morning	Afternoon	Evening
S			
M			
T			
W			
T			
F			
S			

FAMILY TIME FORM 3

Month_____, 19___

S	M	T	W	T	F	S

3

Husband and Wife Together Time

How many times have you heard it said (or said it yourself), "My husband never tells me anything"? I've heard a few variations of that statement in my own home. As I think back over 13 years of marriage, I can remember the many times my wife said, "I wish you would have discussed that with me," or, "I wish you would try a little harder to understand how I feel," or, "Why don't you tell me when things bother you?"

But that's not me. I'm the strong American family man. I earn the living, keep family plans and business in my head and keep my emotions out of sight. In this way I protect my wife by not bothering her with the pressures I feel. After all, isn't that best for her?

Not at all. I found this out the hard way. My attitude over the years damaged our communication.

But I'm not the only man with this problem. According to Dr. James Dobson, in his book *What Wives Wish Their Husbands Knew About Women:* "Too many men do not understand the emotional needs of their wives. They live in a vastly different world with ample frustrations of their own. Either they are unable to put themselves in a woman's place, seeing and feeling what she experiences, or else they are preoccupied with their own work and simply aren't listening. For whatever reason, women have needs which men do not comprehend."[1]

This problem is a reality, and few marriages escape its consequences. H. Norman Wright, in his book *Communication: Key to Your Marriage,* lists a decline in understanding between marriage partners as one of the three major changes taking place in the institution of marriage today. Mr. Wright goes on to say, "Decline of understanding and lack of communication go together."[2]

If communication is the key to a marriage—and most family specialists agree that it is—then learning to understand and communicate with one another should be the number one priority in building a Christian family.

I must admit that for many years this was not very high on my list of priorities, and our marriage showed it. My wife and I never doubted our love for one another. We liked each other's company and talked a lot. But working out problems, that was something else. When we attempted to do so, we invariably ended in angry shouting matches. My wife would claim, "You don't care about my feelings or even try to understand me." My defense would be, "Those feelings are ridiculous! You're not thinking logically!" Rarely did we turn over any new stones. The same problems came up again and again.

The communication problems in my own marriage and the cutting edge of God's Word finally brought me to a place where I said to my wife, "Honey, I'm sorry I have been insensitive to your needs for so many years. But that's past. You and our marriage relationship are now my first priority."

A Love that Listens

I believe the Scripture that cut deepest into my thick skin of marital insensitivity was Ephesians 5:25: "And you husbands, show the same kind of love to your wives as Christ showed to the church when he died for her" (*TLB*).

The blade sank deep and it hurt. I did not show a sacrificial love to my wife. I was not the servant-leader the Scriptures talked about. The kind of love I showed to my wife was based more on my needs than hers. I prided myself in being a good family man. After all, didn't I spend lots of time with the children, playing with them, teaching them? Family togetherness was my specialty. I even wrote books about it. Our family read together, never missed a Family Night, and participated in a lot of other interesting family activities. That, I told myself, really showed my wife I loved her. Wasn't that enough?

No, it wasn't. Although my wife appreciated the things I did with the family, some of her individual needs were not being met. What she really wanted was for me to focus on her needs and problems—to say in some concrete ways, "I care deeply about *your* feelings and want to understand and communicate with *you*. Our relationship is the most important thing in the world to me."

How was I going to meet my wife's needs? Were there

some specific things I could do to show Janet I cared and was going to make a diligent effort to understand her, as Peter urges husbands to do (see 1 Pet. 3:7)?

I had an idea that I shared with my wife. "What would you think," I asked, "if we set aside a time each week to be together alone? We could discuss various things like books, ideas, and problems. We could really work on trying to understand each other's thoughts and feelings. We could also read and discuss a Scripture portion and pray together."

"I really like the idea," my wife replied. "I think a time like that could become very important to us."

Structuring the Time

The following Tuesday evening was our first together time. We tucked the girls in bed early with a lot of books, threatened their lives if they got up, and sat down at the dining room table for our sharing time.

That first night we discussed what we would do during these times together. Here is the approach we decided to use. First we discuss from a book we have selected. Next we have a general discussion and planning time. Our last activity is to share a Scripture passage and pray together.

Our only real preparation for these times together, other than to jot down things we would like to discuss, is to read and take a few notes on the chapter of a book we have selected to read. We find it very helpful to discuss books together. This not only gives us something interesting to talk about, but also provides us ideas and information that strengthen our marriage.

During these together times I personally have learned a great deal from Dr. Dobson's book *What Wives Wish Their Husbands Knew About Women.* I have received many insights into my wife's feelings and needs. I enthusiastically brought my new bits of knowledge to our together time and asked my wife, "Is this true? Is that really the way you feel?"

She assured me that Dr. Dobson was accurate and shared some of her personal feelings on the subject. Many times we thought of specific examples where lack of communication about certain needs caused problems in our marriage.

We do not limit our reading to books about marriage. Recently we read and discussed Letha Scanzoni's *Sex Is a Parent Affair* so that we would be better prepared to teach our children about sex. We also recommend these books for husbands and wives to discuss together: *Communication: Key to Your Marriage,* by H. Norman Wright; *Caring Enough to Confront,* by David Augsburger; *Tough and Tender,* by Joyce Landorf; *Hide or Seek,* by James Dobson; and *Help, I'm a Parent,* by Bruce Narramore.

The second part of our time together, general sharing, is very informal. We simply discuss whatever we currently feel is important. Many times we jot things down during the week so we won't forget them. Some couples might want to compile a list of things to discuss and cover one or two items each week.

Next we go over the family calendar (see chapter 2), and plan the week's activities. This is a very important exercise for us. Before we started doing this, Saturday would arrive with me thinking we were going to do one thing and my wife under the impression we were going to do something else. At times this caused conflict. Now there are few surprises. We plan our family activities in advance. One thing we always plan is Family Night. We talk about what we are going to do, who will be responsible for gathering materials and so forth.

We conclude our time together by reading a section of Scripture and praying. We do no advance preparation for this. We simply read a Scripture passage (we are now going through Ephesians) and discuss what that Scripture says to us personally or what implications it has for our marriage. Many times the reading of the Scripture will open topics that we discuss at length.

After our Scripture reading we bring up things we need to pray about. I can't emphasize enough how much this means to us, to pray about family decisions or problems and to pray for the children and one another. My wife commented the other day that before we started praying together "sometimes we were asking God for different solutions to the same problem." Now as we sit, face to face, praying together, there is a sense of mutual commitment to common goals, to Christ, and to each other.

Does It Work?

I am not saying that a husband and wife together time of one or two hours a week is a magic formula for instant communication or a cure-all for marital problems. Nothing is that simple, certainly not the process of building good patterns of communication. But I do wish to emphasize that my wife and I find regular times together to be a very valuable tool that helps us grow closer to one another and to God. The destructive angry quarrels which characterized our former way of handling conflict have virtually been eliminated. We still have conflict, to be sure, but we now deal with it in a more loving, understanding way.

My wife puts it this way, "Our together times give me

the confidence to bring up those things I dread to talk about. I feel we can talk about anything without having a quarrel."

For me this weekly period is a kind of practice session in communication. It helps me develop the skills, attitudes and sensitivity that enables me to communicate effectively in other relationships.

A husband and wife together time is not the only way to build good communication, but it works for us and some of you might find it helpful. The important thing is that we give our marriage the same top billing that God gives it in Scripture. I am convinced that, if we do our part, God will give us the strength and wisdom to build beautiful marriages—the foundation of Christian families.

Footnotes

1. James Dobson, *What Wives Wish Their Husbands Knew About Women* (Wheaton: Tyndale House Publishers, 1975), p. 13.
2. H. Norman Wright, *Communication: Key to Your Marriage* (Glendale, Regal Books, G/L Publications, 1974), Intro.

4

Developing Family Values

My wife and I have in our minds a picture of the type of persons we want our children to become. We would like them to have a deep personal commitment to Christ, to be growing Christians, to be emotionally stable, to have a real love and concern for others, to be well educated, to have successful marriages and families, and to achieve in areas that are important to them.

These are values—Christian values we feel—that Janet and I hold, and we are vitally interested that our children come to hold these same values. I'm sure you have your own set of expectations, hopes and dreams for your children. These are your values—things you feel are important.

The values we hold serve as standards for our behavior. They shape our attitudes, our ways of judging things. For example, if we value honesty then we will not steal or lie.

If moral purity is a value then we will not participate in sex outside of marriage. Because we are Christians our values are based on biblical principles.

When we arrange our values in an order of priority, we have a value system. Even though we are Christians and believe in many of the same things, our value systems may be different because we arrange values in a different order of importance.

Deciding on Values

In my Creative Home Teaching Seminars, I ask parents to list their five top values and rank them in the order of importance. For most parents this is the first time they have ever thought through exactly what values they would like to communicate to their children.

This can be a very helpful exercise. Listing our values in the order of priority enables us to clarify them to ourselves and our children. From this set of values we can develop spiritual goals for ourselves and for our children.

I would like to suggest that you and your spouse work together on the following project.

I have listed the 10 values most frequently mentioned as important by parents in my seminars. At the bottom of the column is space for you to write additional values of your own.

Read through the list and number the values in order of importance. Enter the number of the "rank" column opposite the appropriate value. Number one will be the value you feel is most important. The value you prize second highest will be number two. Use this procedure to rank all the values on the list.

When you have completed ranking the values find an appropriate Scripture to go with each one. Then ask yourself the following two questions: (1) What am I presently doing to teach these values to my children? (2) What can I do to teach these values more effectively?

VALUE	RANK	SCRIPTURE
ENDURANCE (Perseverance, sticking to a task)		
PATIENCE (Making allowances for others)		
TRUST (Faith in God for everything)		
LOVE (Love of God and others)		
WISDOM (Application of God's Word to life)		
SELF-ESTEEM (Accepting oneself)		
SELF-DISCIPLINE (Correction or regulation of oneself for the sake of improvement)		
HONESTY (Integrity in all of life)		
KINDNESS (Treating others in a loving way)		
_____		
_____		
_____		

A United Front

It is very important for parents to present a united front to their children. As Christian parents we need to know what values we want our children to internalize and then be diligent in communicating these important truths to them.

When parents do not agree on specific values, children become confused. A recent study of Kent State students on changing family values showed that young people whose parents did not agree on mutual religious or political preferences or on their life goals, were more likely to hold radical attitudes toward the family, than those whose parents held clearcut values.[1]

There has probably never been a time in our country when parents, even Christian parents, were less sure of what they believe. As a result we see a generation of youth who are virtually without a value system. I believe Alvin Toffler's analysis of our nation is correct. He writes: "Seldom has a single nation shown greater confusion over its sexual values. Yet the same might be said for other kinds of values as well. America is tortured by uncertainty [over] money, property, law and order, race, religion, God, family, and self."[2]

Our children need to hear us say, "Here is where we stand and we want you to stand with us." Our Christian values should be communicated in a coherent, loving, understanding but unbending way.

Janet and I want to help our children walk through the stages of their development to a mature Christian conscience. This means working ourselves out of a job. We have a major commitment to Heidi, Liesl and Bridget not merely to pass on a set of rules and regulations, but to enable them to internalize a thoroughly Christian value system—to develop a solid, growing faith of their own.

A Family Constitution

However, a prerequisite to helping our children acquire a mature Christian conscience is for us, as parents, to know where *we* stand, to live out our values and communicate them clearly and unashamedly to them. We feel it is important to stand with Joshua and say boldly, "As for me and my family, we will serve the Lord" (Josh. 24:15, *TLB*).

A close friend of mine, Phil Moreno, recently took such a stand with his family. Phil has really grown since he became a Christian six years ago. He is the spiritual leader of his wife and five children and a committed leader in the church. For Phil family life seemed to be going great until he encountered a problem a couple of months ago. Phil's fourteen-year-old son, Phil Jr., approached him excitedly one day and said, "Hey Dad, I've got a chance to go to an Oakland Raider ball game with a friend and his family next Sunday morning. Can I go? It won't cost me anything."

Phil felt that this was an exceptional opportunity for his son to see a pro game so he gave his consent. The following week Phil Jr. came to his dad with a similar request. This time he wanted to go skating on Sunday morning with the same family. Phil was unhappy with the request but decided to leave the decision up to his son. "Son," he said, "I really want you to go to church with the family but I'm going to leave that decision up to you."

"Good, I'm going skating," he replied.

Phil was deeply hurt. He felt certain his son would make the right decision. During the next three agonizing days Phil reflected on his role as a father and as the spiritual leader of his home. He spent eight hours looking up Scriptures regarding family life. The finished product was a comprehensive Family Constitution that covered everything from attitudes to the role of the father, mother, and children in the family. Certain things were spelled out in detail, such as, "The whole family will attend church on Sundays except in the case of sickness."

The Family Constitution was read and discussed on Family Night. Usually Family Nights at the Moreno home are happy, fun-filled affairs. Not this Family Night. It was one of painful soul-searching. A lot of tears were shed. But as a result of the family's struggle and intro-spection there is a new strength, a greater sense of solidarity. And even Phil Jr.'s attitude about it is positive.

God rewarded the Moreno family in a very significant way as Phil stood firm on his values. I really feel that God will reward all parents who will stand with Joshua and say, "As for me and my family, we will serve the Lord."

Three Ways to Communicate Christian Values

How did Joshua communicate religious values to his children? He must have listened closely when Moses explained to the Hebrew parents God's plan for teaching religious values in the family.

Mothers and fathers were told that they were first to *model* God's laws for their children—that is, to teach by example. In Deuteronomy 6:5,6 we read, "And thou shalt love the Lord thy God with all thine heart. . . . And these words, which I command thee this day, shall be in thine heart."

Not only were they to have these laws in their own hearts but they were told, *"Teach* them diligently unto thy

34

children" (Deut. 6:7). The phrase "teach diligently" suggests a structured teaching situation, a time set aside by parents to share God's Word with their children.

Hebrew parents were also to use informal situations to teach God's values to their children. They were to *talk* as they sat in the house, as they lay down, as they got up, and as they walked (see Deut. 6:7-9).

The following sketch shows how these principles fit together to make a very effective teaching life-style—a comprehensive approach to the matter of teaching Christian values to our children.

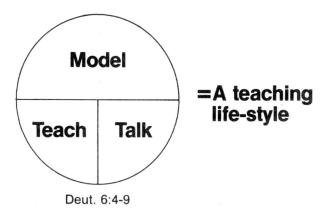

Deut. 6:4-9

Janet and I find that these principles work. They are very useful tools that help us build Christian values in our children. We have a team approach to teaching the children these values. We both have responsibilities for Family Night and other family times. We plan together weekly. However, we both feel very strongly that I am the spiritual leader of our home and responsible for the teaching.

We feel that as the head and leader-servant of my wife

(1 Cor. 11:3; Eph. 5:21-33), it is my responsibility to give direction to the teaching of Christian values in our home. As the father-leader-teacher portrayed in God's Word I must see that the job gets done!

I admit that teaching Christian values effectively to our children is a difficult task. But I believe God wants to enable every parent to do so. This book may help. I do not offer any magic formulas, but lots of ideas to help you communicate to your children that which is in your heart.

Footnotes

1. "Parent-Child Interaction and Changing Family Values: A Multivariate Analysis," *Journal of Marriage and Family,* February, 1974, p. 118.
2. Alvin Toffler, *Future Shock* (New York: Random House, 1971), p. 303.

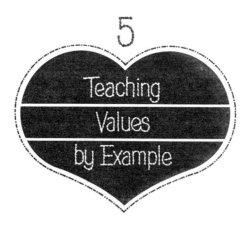

5

Teaching Values by Example

"And what did you do at school today Bridget?" asked Liesl our nine-year-old daughter, as she skillfully guided the dinner conversation, making sure each family member felt special.

Janet laughed as she told me about the incident, which happened while I was on a trip. "She sounded so much like you it was hilarious."

Unfortunately Liesl does not always mirror my good qualities. Like the day Liesl and Heidi were trading cutting remarks. I stepped in to referee and said, "I realize you are upset with one another, but couldn't you use kinder words to express your feelings?"

"But Dad," Liesl replied solemnly, "that's the way you talk to us when you're upset."

I quickly reminded the girls that I was working on that

problem and asked, "Don't you think I have made some improvement in the last couple of years?" Expecting to be reaffirmed I was a little shocked when Liesl quickly answered, "No."

I defended myself a little more, mumbled something like "Nobody's perfect" and walked away, reminded once again that at times my actions speak so loudly that no one can hear my words.

In both cases I taught very effectively by example. At the dinner table Liesl showed she had learned to be thoughtful and sensitive to the feelings of others. Later Liesl showed she had learned another lesson well—to respond with harsh words when upset or angry.

Liesl is learning values in the most basic way, by the example Janet and I set. Research has long pointed out the awesome potential of parental example. Dr. Vladimir de Lissavoy of Penn State University writes: "Research on the attainment of moral perspectives, on observational learning and sexual development clearly indicate that parental influence in the establishment of value priorities is related to certain conditions. Most crucial are the standards parents hold for their own behavior and the clarity of their explanation of the behavior they expect from their children."[1]

Children Identify with Parents

Why are our values so crucial to the moral development of our children? Because of a process called "identification." "Both consciously and unconsciously, children want to be like their mothers and fathers. This process is known as identification or internalization. In it children gradually take on their parents' attitudes and values; they become increasingly like their parents."[2]

38

I'm sure you see this "identification" at work in your home as Janet and I do in ours. Isn't it amazing how accurately our children reflect our attitudes? Sometimes this makes us feel very proud, but other times we feel like crawling under a rug. Our children identify with us, mirror our values and "develop an image of who and how they think they ought to be. This *ideal self,* as it is known, consists of all the values learned early in life. . . . By adolescence this ideal self or 'ego ideal' is well formed. While new ideals may be added, the basic content and attitudes are firmly entrenched; this ego ideal will serve as a measuring rod throughout the rest of life."[3]

During adolescence our children will rethink many of these values as they develop a value system of their own, but the basic pattern is set.

Biblical Examples

Modeling or teaching by example is deeply rooted in God's Word. It was Jesus' basic way of training twelve men to revolutionize the world. He "selected twelve of them to be his regular companions" (Mark 3:14, *TLB*). Jesus taught His disciples the quality of humility and servanthood, not by delivering a twenty-minute lecture, but by demonstration.

Jesus washed His disciples' feet to show them in an unforgettable manner that they were to serve Christ and the church. "And since I, the Lord and Teacher, have washed your feet, you ought to wash each other's feet. I have given you an example to follow; do as I have done to you" (John 13:14,15, *TLB*).

Early church leaders also understood the advantages of teaching by example. Peter urged leaders, "Don't be tyrants, but lead them by your good example" (1 Pet. 5:3,

TLB). And assuming the powerful influence of a parent's example on his children, Paul says, "Follow God's example in everything you do just as a much loved child imitates his father" (Eph. 5:1, *TLB*).

I like the way *The Living Bible* paraphrases this verse, for "a much loved child" is more likely to follow the example of his parents than one who does not feel loved. When a child feels loved and accepted, he will want to be like his parents. This is an extremely important point to remember. In fact our success in teaching Christian values depends on the quality of the relationship we have with our children.

Relationship: The Fertile Soil for Teaching

This says to me that a high priority in my life must be to show my children in some very concrete ways that I love them. How can I do that? By spending time with them, playing, listening, talking, and being concerned with *their interests and needs.*

I have listened to some authorities say that children do not want their parents to play with them, but I have never seen any evidence to support this. On the contrary it has been my experience that children enjoy playing with their parents. Playing together creates a feeling of closeness that is very real to children and lets children know in a tangible way that their parents are interested in *their* world.

One evening last summer I arrived home about 10:30 P.M. after a speaking engagement. As I walked in the door, I heard the thundering of four little hoofs and turned just in time to see that I was about to be pounced on by Heidi and Liesl.

Slowly picking myself up off the floor, I asked that

inevitable question, "What are you doing out of bed?"

"Oh Dad," replied Heidi excitedly, "you've just got to see our new cardboard box forts. They're really neat."

So we made the pilgrimage to the construction site— Heidi and Liesl's room. There stood two magnificent cardboard appliance box forts. For the next thirty minutes I served as a cardboard box consulting engineer. "How do you think we can hang curtains in the windows Dad? Do you know where there are any scraps of carpet we could use for the floor? How can we make bookshelves in our forts?" The barrage of questions kept coming. Finally Heidi said, "Thanks a lot Dad. You sure know a lot about cardboard boxes!"

Cardboard boxes, wrestling matches, hikes, ball games, silly jokes, stories, pillow fights—such activities are all doors to our children's world. We can enter through these doors, go beyond the walls that many times keep generations apart, and build the kind of relationships with our children that will make them responsive to our teaching.

Because Heidi, Liesl and Bridget know that Janet and I are vitally interested in their world, because they feel "much loved," they are open to what we think is important for their lives—God's Word.

Teaching by Demonstration

I learned what most people, especially parents of teenagers, feel is a very dangerous occupation by simply observing a skilled professional for 30 hours. I sat in the back seat of a Driver Education car while a driving instructor demonstrated with real live high school students how to teach teenagers to drive. At first I thought the job was impossible, but as I continued to watch this patient and skilled man hour after hour I began to pick up clues to how he survived. Between students he passed on to me little survival tips—why he said something or handled a situation in a certain way. After 30 hours I felt confident that I could handle a Driver Education job and even have fun doing it.

During the next three years I thoroughly enjoyed teaching over 500 high school students how to drive. My teaching techniques were patterned very closely after those of the instructor I observed. Since that time I have had a great respect for the potential of teaching by demonstration.

There are many exciting opportunities to teach by demonstration in every home. We often demonstrate values informally, and this is very important. But it is also important occasionally to *plan* to teach certain Christian values by demonstration.

Some time ago Janet said to me, "Wayne, you know the girls never see us having our personal devotions. Maybe that is one reason why we're having such a hard time motivating them to have their own." I'd never thought of it that way before, but it made sense. My wife had her devotions after the children left for school and I had mine before the family got up in the morning. As a result, the children never saw us having our quiet times with God.

Janet and I decided to demonstrate the value of a regular quiet time with God. We use several approaches. On occasion, we have our devotions when our children can observe us. At times we have silent devotions together as a family and then share what God has said to us through His Word. At least once a week at the dinner hour I ask a family member to share what he experienced in his quiet time that morning. This not only gives us a chance to discuss spiritual things but also says to our children, "We value our quiet times and want to help you experience the same benefits that come from personal devotions."

Even with this emphasis we found that our children were not regular in their devotions. This was not because they were disinterested but because they would sometimes forget in the rush and confusion of the morning.

One solution to that problem was to help them structure into their morning schedule a time for their devotions. Now, each morning after they make their beds, before they dress, they have their devotions. This works out very well. Just this morning Heidi came into my office at about a quarter to eight and said, "Guess what I read this morning for my devotions. Eight chapters of Ruth. It's really interesting. The only reason I stopped was because I ran out of time."

I had to laugh. That wasn't devotions, it was a Bible marathon. But the point is this: our children value personal devotions because we demonstrate in a very visible way that they are important to us.

I would like to suggest a simple three-step process that Janet and I find helpful in demonstrating values to our children. We like to call it "Demonstrating Values in 3-D." Here's how it works:

Decide. First we decide what value we would like to demonstrate. In the preceding example it was personal devotions.

Develop. This involves two areas. First we must develop the value in our own lives. We find out what God's Word has to say about it. We pray and meditate on a Scripture passage pertaining to the value and then ask God to make changes in our life. When we wanted to demonstrate the value of personal devotions to our children we first had to strengthen that area in our own lives.

Demonstrate. When our own experience is squared away, then we can plan ways in which to demonstrate that value to our children. We demonstrated the value of personal devotions to our children in several ways: by our own example, by helping them develop a regular time, and by periodically asking them to share what they had learned.

I would like to challenge you to do a demonstration project with your children. First *decide* what value you would like to demonstrate to your children. In chapter 3 I asked you to rank certain values in order of importance. You might want to choose one of those values. Next *develop* that value in your own life. Be specific. List some steps you will take in order to grow in that area. Then *develop* some ways to demonstrate that value to your children. Finally *demonstrate.* Show your children in some very practical ways how that value can be lived out in daily life. You will be amazed how you and your children will grow spiritually by participating in this project.

Seeing Our "Projects" Develop

Teaching by example, whether conscious demonstration or informal day-to-day modeling in the Christian life, is our greatest teaching tool for helping our children develop mature Christian consciences. When our children leave home in young adulthood they will bear the imprint of what they have seen in our lives.

Joyce Landorf, in her book *Tough and Tender,* shares a letter from her son Rick that illustrates from a young adult's point of view the importance of a parent's example:

"Mom,

This is my last Mother's Day at home. This summer you will be sending out the first of your two 'projects' to build a house of his own. I'm not leaving under duress, or just 'to get out' but I am standing firm on my own two feet proud of where I came from.

"For the last twenty years you have been shaping, molding and even cultivating me as your son.

"I have watched your marriage succeed. I have *seen* the unseeable love between you and Dad. I have felt God bring our family together as one unit."[4]

What a tribute to raising children God's way! Janet and I pray that someday Heidi, Liesl and Bridget will be able to say, like Rick, that their parents' example shaped their lives and prepared them for building their own homes.

God expects us to be growing examples to our children, and what God expects God enables. We can trust God, as we open our lives to His Word, to make us Christ-centered examples for our children to follow.

Footnotes

1. Vladimir de Lissavoy, *Today's Child*, vol. 24 (May, 1974), p. 7.
2. Bruce Narramore, *An Ounce of Prevention* (Grand Rapids: Zondervan Publishing House, 1973), p. 72.
3. Narramore, *An Ounce of Prevention*, p. 73.
4. Joyce Landorf, *Tough and Tender* (Old Tappan, N.J.: Fleming H. Revell, 1975), p. 119.

6

Planning
a Regular
Family Night

I recently returned to a church where I had held a Creative Home Teaching Seminar a year before. The occasion was a Family Night Fair. Families in the church set up tables in the gym on which they displayed ideas they had used during the year on their Family Nights. I was amazed as I walked from table to table at the really fine things families did together.

I stopped at one table where there were ten 5″x5″ cards with magazine pictures pasted on them. "There is a Scripture verse that goes with each picture," explained the father of a five-year-old boy. "He has memorized ten verses. He looks at the picture and says the verse. When he learned all ten verses we took him out for ice cream."

Another table caught my eye. This one had lying on it, among other things, an interesting looking scrapbook. "Our children," the mother explained, "made this for their Dad on 'Honor Your Father' Family Night. The children cut out magazine pictures that reminded them

46

of Dad and pasted them in the scrapbook. Then with my help they wrote under each picture a statement about Dad, such as 'Daddy likes camping,' and 'Daddy likes to exercise.' The picture I really think is precious is one of a husband and wife embracing. Under that picture is written the children's statement, 'Mommy loves Daddy.' "

Every table had good, usable projects. "What a way to get ideas," I thought as I observed families busily jotting down notes and asking questions about one another's family nights.

After families made the rounds of Family Night exhibits, everyone sat down for a time of informal sharing and demonstration. One father demonstrated how he used finger puppets on Family Nights. "I was half-hearted when we first started Family Nights," he admitted, "but the kids were so enthusiastic it turned me on."

That's why I'm so excited about Family Nights. I see an ever-increasing number of parents and children having great times on Family Nights while sharing God's Word together.

It's certainly true of our family. We have more fun now than when we started three years ago. We do a lot of other things together, but Family Night is really the highlight of the week.

Your family can have good times together too. You can be creative. God has given you that capacity. If you have not started to do so, I encourage you to establish a regular Family Night. If you already have, the following information will be valuable in helping you improve it.

How to Get Started

Find a Time. This is very important—and difficult.

Family Nights work best if they are the same night each week. But that is impossible with some families, including my own. Another approach is to select the best night each week for the family to be together. Methods may vary, but it is important to commit yourself to one night a week for Family Night. Discipline yourself never to miss.

Find Ideas. Ideas are not as hard to find as you might think. We can be thankful that there are some good family time resources being published. *Family Life Today,* a monthly magazine published by Gospel Light Publications, has four family time ideas each month, plus other helpful materials. My book, *Good Times for Your Family,* has over 100 family time ideas, many of which can be used for Family Nights.[1] This book also has a section on how to create your own family times. I am very impressed by the ideas in Elva Anson's *How to Keep the Family that Prays Together from Falling Apart.*[2]

Create Your Own Family Nights. Creating Family Nights is not as difficult as it first may seem. The basic requirements for a Family Night are quite simple. You need a topic, a Scripture passage and an activity. God's Word is filled with possible Family Night topics. Each one of the Beatitudes in Matthew 5 would work well. In Galatians 5, Paul lists the fruits of the Spirit, each of which would make a good Family Night topic. The book of Proverbs is loaded with good ideas!

Family Nights can be built around special family needs or problems. Could your children use some instruction on how to handle money? You might create a Family Night entitled "Money Matters." Scripture passages you might use include Matthew 25:14-30, and 2 Cor. 9:6-15.

Are your children careless about personal hygiene?

You might entitle a Family Night "Your Body, the Temple of God," using 1 Corinthians 6:19,20 as a Scripture passage.

List some of your family's needs or problems. Would they make good Family Night topics?

Special events such as birthdays, spiritual birthdays, anniversaries, graduations and special recognitions can make memorable Family Nights.

Many good Family Nights can be built around holidays. For the last two years we have used the Family Night prior to Halloween to carve pumpkins and discuss what the Bible has to say about fear and witchcraft.

We also use pre-Thanksgiving Family Nights to prepare for that holiday. We study some Scriptures on thankfulness, make "Let's be thankful" posters and design place mats and napkins for Thanksgiving Day.

Other Family Night Ideas

You can get ideas for activities to go with your Family Night topics from various sources. Game and craft books have activities that can be adapted to your theme. In my book *Good Times for Your Family* there are 24 basic games and activities that can be used with your Family Night topics.

Parents of preschoolers will like *202 Things to Do,*[3] and *158 Things to Make,*[4] by Margaret Self. These books give guidance to activities that will help you create enjoyable Family Nights around certain topics or Scripture passages.

Other families who have Family Nights are good sources of ideas. Get together with them occasionally and share experiences. You might even want to have a Family Night Fair.

To help you get started let me share some of our Family Nights with you. These are just kernel ideas. Expand them, adapt them or do whatever you feel is necessary to make them fit your family.

Honor Child Night. This works great with our children. They love to be honored. Set aside a Family Night to honor each child. Call your Family Night "(*child's name*) Night."

Have your family make a flower for the one being honored. Draw a flower on construction paper and cut out the center and petals. Write your child's name on the center piece and give each family member one of the petals. Have each person write on his petal what he appreciates about the honoree and give it to him. Then ask the one being honored to paste his flower piece by piece on a sheet of construction paper and keep it as a reminder of his family's love for him.

Share with your child how he is special and important to the family. Be specific. What makes him special? In what important ways does he contribute to family life?

Show some slides or other pictures of your child. Tell an interesting story about him. Tell the story of his life from birth until the present using his baby book as an outline. Tell him why you chose his name and the meaning of it. Let him select the special dessert.

Monument to a Miracle. After God performed that great miracle of stopping the Jordan River so that the children of Israel could enter the Promised Land, Joshua told 12 men to build a monument to that miracle so "that this may be a sign among you, when your children ask in time to come, 'What do those stones mean to you?' " (Joshua 4:6, *RSV*). Israelite parents were to answer the questions by telling the story of that great miracle.

Has God performed miracles in your family? Remember that any answer to prayer is a miracle. Have a Family Night commemorating the miracles God has performed in your family.

First read Joshua 4. Next discuss some things God has done for your family. Select what you feel is the most important miracle God performed in your household and build a monument as a reminder. You might want to glue 12 small rocks together.

Another idea is to start a "Monument to a Miracle" scrapbook. Each time God performs a miracle for your family, put something in the notebook to remind you of what God has done. This could be a picture, an object or a written account of what happened.

Close your Family Night by having each person thank God for the great things he has done for your family.

Spiritual Birthdays. We use several Family Nights each year to celebrate spiritual birthdays. Our children are very enthusiastic about these special celebrations of their new birth.

Here are some things you can do. Share with your child the importance of his new birth. Use this opportunity to review the significance of the following Scriptures: John 3:1-15; Ephesians 2:1-10; 2 Corinthians 5:11-21; Ephesians 6:10-18; 1 John 5:11-13.

Each parent may give a personal testimony of his new birth, how he made the decision, the difference it made in his life, some of his struggles, defeats and victories since.

Make a birthday cake with a candle for each year of your child's new life. Have your child blow out the candles. Sing "Happy Birthday." Give your child an appropriate present such as a new Bible, a Bible study guide or a Christian novel.

Have each person write a special Scripture verse on an index card and give it to the one having the spiritual birthday.

Ideal-Parent/Ideal-Child Night. We find it helpful at times to spend a Family Night discussing our relationships with one another. Here is an idea that will open up good communication about family roles.

Have your children make a list of things they feel make an ideal parent while you and your spouse make a list of things you feel make an ideal child. When the lists are completed, read them aloud and discuss them. When you have discussed the ideals, decide together on the five most important things that make an ideal parent and the five most important things that make an ideal child. Write these lists on separate sheets of paper and try to find Scriptures to go with each item. Challenge each family member to live up to these ideals.

Family Night Field Trips. We find it fun to have Family Night field trips. Here are some ideas you can use:

• Visit a fire station. When you return home talk about safety. Read 1 Corinthians 6:19,20. Could this verse apply to safety? How? Map out a fire escape plan for your home and have a fire drill.

• Visit a police station. Later read and discuss 1 Peter 2:13-17. What should our attitude be toward all kinds of authority? Write a letter of thanks to the police station.

• Visit a farm. Discuss why God made so many different kinds of animals. Read Genesis 1:24,25. Have family members either pantomime or draw a picture of an animal of their choice.

• Visit a graveyard. Read the epitaphs on tombstones. Discuss death. Discuss important points in 1 Corinthians 15.

• Visit a government office. Talk about the importance of those who manage the affairs of our state and nation. Read 1 Timothy 2:1-3. Pray for our national leaders, especially the president. Have each person write a personal note to the president. Thank him for the work he does for us and let him know you are praying for him.

Questions About Family Nights

Now I want to share with you answers to the five most common questions I am asked about Family Nights.

1. *What one thing do you feel is the key to a successful Family Night?*

I would have to say participation. Let's face it: people, especially children, like to participate, to be part of the action. I find that our Family Nights work best if *everyone* has something to do. One person might lead a game, while another person reads the Scripture or leads the discussion. Another family member might prepare materials for an art project while still another leads prayer, leads in a song, or serves dessert. Sometimes we assign family members specific tasks and at other times the children just "do their own thing," such as pantomime, tell a joke, or lead a game. Again, and I cannot emphasize this enough, *everyone needs something to do.*

2. *We have only young preschool children. Should we start Family Nights or wait until they are older?*

Start now, even if you have a six-month-old baby. Babies will soon sense that this is a special time with Mom and Dad together. Show your baby large pictures from a Bible story book and talk about them even though he cannot understand. In this way just a few minutes with your child will help you establish early a tradition of home-centered Christian education.

When you have small children, remember to keep Family Night simple, short, and fun. Preschoolers have very short attention spans. A Bible story, a game or craft activity and a special dessert will usually be enough.

And don't forget the obvious. Your children will be delighted if you play such games as Hide and Seek, London Bridge Is Falling Down, and Ring Around the Rosy with them. Remember other standbys, like coloring, pasting, drawing and clay modeling.

3. Is it possible to have successful Family Nights with teenagers?

There are two main obstacles to having Family Nights with teenagers—time and interest. Most parents of teenagers I talk to say that it is really difficult to get the family together at one time. I do know some families with teenagers that have successful Family Nights. Others have to settle for catching snatches of family time when they can.

It is possible to have family time with teenagers, but you may have to be creative to fit it into your family situation. Maybe Family Nights as such will not be best for you. You might like to take a more informal approach. Discuss this with your teenagers. Ask them what they feel would be worthwhile and then design family times to meet the needs of your particular family.

4. Can a family with children of widespread ages have successful Family Nights?

Yes. I believe any family, even those with a widespread in children's ages can have successful Family Nights. Of course the larger the age span between the youngest and oldest child, the more difficult it is to meet everyone's needs and interests.

It is important to try to make everyone feel a part of

Family Night. On some Family Nights use material geared primarily to the younger children and at other times use approaches that your older children will enjoy. Encourage the older children to help the younger ones. Christian sensitivity and tolerance are developed as the family works together on Family Night across age and generation lines.

5. *How long should a Family Night last?*

This depends to some extent on the ages of your children. A Family Night with young children might only last 10 to 20 minutes. Some parents tell me that their Family Nights last as long as two hours. We usually start our Family Night at 7:00 and it is over at 8:00.

We find it best to finish Family Night at bedtime. If we end early we play a game, read a book or do some other joint activity that can keep the whole family busy until bedtime.

Now that you have lots of information on Family Nights, why not try one with your family. I'm convinced that you can have many good times with your family if you will use this creative approach to sharing your lives and God's Word together.

Footnotes

1. Wayne E. Rickerson, *Good Times for Your Family* (Glendale, Calif.: Regal Books, G/L Publications, 1976).
2. Elva Anson, *How to Keep the Family that Prays Together from Falling Apart* (Chicago: Moody Press, 1975).
3. Margaret Self, *202 Things to Do* (Glendale, Calif.: Regal Books, G/L Publications, 1968).
4. Margaret Self, *158 Things to Make* (Glendale, Calif.: Regal Books, G/L Publications, 1971).

7

Creating Family Unity at the Dinner Hour

Marjorie Holmes, in *You and I and Yesterday*, laments the tragic loss of the dinner hour in American homes:

"Whatever happened to the family dinner hour? or 'Supper' as we called it in our small town? That time at the end of the day when everybody was summoned to wash up and sit down together to share a common meal. A time not only to eat but to talk to each other, even if you sometimes quarreled. A time and place where you could laugh, joke, exchange ideas, tell stories, dump your troubles. (Yes, and learn your manners.)

"Surely its disappearance has a lot to do with the much lamented disintegration of the American family."[1]

Does Mrs. Holmes have reason to be alarmed? Is the family meal losing importance in American homes?

Yes, according to a study cited in *Today's Child* magazine. Dr. Paul A. Fine, psychological consultant to several food companies, exploded several myths about the American family's eating habits. One common myth he attacks is that the family eats together regularly:

"The myth: Americans eat breakfasts and dinners together as a family, drawing spiritual as well as nutritional sustenance from the shared ritual.

"The reality: Fine's survey revealed that families tend to sit down to dinner together no more than three times a week and often less frequently. The dining rite is generally completed within 20 minutes. Three out of four families do not breakfast together; many skip breakfast entirely."[2]

Now why all this fuss about the family eating together? Is it really that important to family life? I believe it is. What happens when the family eats together—especially at the dinner hour—is an extremely important part of building family unity and teaching Christian values. By conversation at the dinner hour, listening, sharing, communicating ideas and dreams, the family circle is drawn tighter with love and understanding.

Chinese families have long looked at family talk during mealtime as a deterrent to juvenile delinquency and a vehicle for communicating values.

"In our homes," a Chinese clergyman explained to author Oscar Schisgall, "we *talk* to one another and enjoy our talk. From what I have seen, I think American homes are losing the love of good family conversation and companionship. Families eat together, yes; but immediately after the meal the children run out to seek their friends in the street."[3]

In China, America, Africa, all around the world the

family dinner has been a focal point of family life. In many homes this is the only regular family time available. James H. S. Bossard, a keen student of family life, reports that the majority of family conversation occurs in the dining room, that this is, in fact, the "social center" of the household.[4]

Suppertime at the Rickersons

In our home the dinner hour is certainly the hub of family activities. Janet and I feel that this time, usually from 5:30 to 6:30, is a key tool in helping us build a Christian home.

Janet always sets the atmosphere by making the table look attractive. Over a period of years she has purchased a variety of table accessories, such as place mats, candles, napkins and centerpieces. That "extra touch" Janet gives to decorating the table says to the rest of us, "I really care—I want you to enjoy our time together."

And we do enjoy these times. A lot of things happen at our dinner hour. I won't say our meals are without hassles—we have our share—but the positive things that happen overshadow any negative disruptions.

We try to keep conversation positive, lively and interesting. Janet is an avid reader; so many times she will share some bit of information from a book she is reading. The children are often bursting with exciting information from school.

I plan methods to help stimulate our table talk. When the meal is over, we spend the rest of the dinner hour doing something together. We always try to have some time of spiritual thought. At times I ask a family member to share insights they received from their personal devotions that day. About once a week we discuss a question from our question box. Family members are encouraged to place in the box questions about the Bible or Christian living they want to discuss.

One of our favorite ways of sharing spiritual thoughts is to read and discuss together a chapter from a Christian book. The "Jungle Doctor" series by Paul White is very popular with our family.[5] Bridget especially enjoys the "Pete and Penny" series.[6] Several years ago we started our dinner hour tradition of reading aloud by going through the "Little House" series by Laura Ingalls Wilder.[7] We have been enthusiastic about family reading ever since.

I would like to suggest a valuable resource for those of you who would like to read together as a family. *Honey for a Child's Heart*, by Gladys Hunt, gives important insights as to how good literature can help build family unity and help mold the character of children.[8] Mrs. Hunt gives a comprehensive list of good books and the approximate ages at which these books can be enjoyed by children.

How to Build Dinner Hour Togetherness

A little planning will help you make the most out of your dinner hour. Not that everything needs to be structured—you should leave plenty of room for things to "just happen." Some simple planning, however, can increase the quality of the time you spend together.

Why not discuss this chapter with your spouse? Are you happy with the way things are going? Are there some activities mentioned in this chapter you would like to try? Set some goals. Could you have a "dinner hour" once a week? Twice a week? Would you like to try reading together?

To help you plan good times for your dinner hour,

Janet and I have compiled a list of activities our family enjoys.

Word of the Week. Each week have a family member research in a Bible dictionary and share the meaning of a Bible word, such as exile, high priest, Emmanuel, Christian, atonement, apostle, gospel, fast, Crete, revelation, etc. The person should read a verse in which the word is used. You might want to have each person start a dictionary of his own by writing the word and its meaning in a notebook or on an index card.

Question Box. Decorate a container of some kind and call it your "Question Box." Have each person write three Bible-related questions they would like to discuss on slips of paper. Put these in the box. Draw and discuss one question periodically. Encourage family members to put new questions in the box continually.

"What's the Meaning, Father?" (Deut. 6:20). Are you ready for this one, Dad? Occasionally let your children ask you a question. Your children might ask, "What do you think is the most important verse in the Bible?" If the question is difficult and will take some research, give them a "questions check" and answer it the next day.

Give Mom and Dad the Word. This activity will probably be very popular with your children. Let them give you a word and then you respond with a story from your past based on that word. For example, if your child gives you the word "Christmas," you could tell about an especially exciting Christmas you remember from your childhood.

Share a Thought from Private Devotions. About once a week I ask someone in our family to share a thought from his personal devotions. I find it best to make the request before the dinner hour so the person can have his devotions if he has not already done so.

What About Your Day? Say a family member's name and a time of day, such as "John—11:00 A.M." John then must respond with a detailed account of what he was doing at that time.

Ask and Answer. Select a passage of Scripture to read. Tell family members that, after the Scripture has been read aloud, each person must be ready to ask and answer a question. Read the passage and have each person close his Bible. One family member starts this activity by asking the person on his left a question about the Scripture. That person answers and then asks the person on his left a question. Continue this procedure until each family member has asked and answered a question.

Place Mat Fun. A family can have many good times at the dinner table by working together on place mats. Use shelf, construction or even typing paper for place mats. Here are some activities you can use for place mat fun:

1. Have each person draw a picture of a Bible verse or story.

2. Select a "thought of the day" and have each person write it at the top of his place mat. Thoughts can be Bible topics such as salvation, Jesus, Holy Spirit, sin, Satan, grace, patience, humility, etc. Give family members five minutes to write down all their thoughts about that word. Discuss the word as family members share their thoughts.

3. Fold your place mats in fourths. Have each person draw a continuous Bible story using the four panels.

4. Scramble the letters of a Bible word. For example, sin scrambled might look like this, *nis.* Have family members exchange place mats and try to figure out the scrambled words. Discuss the various words.

5. Select one family member to draw a picture of a

Scripture verse or Bible story while the rest of the family tries to guess what he is drawing.

6. Have family members make an acrostic out of a Bible word. To make an acrostic you letter a word vertically on your place mat and then think of a word that starts with each letter. New words should be associated with the acrostic word, as shown below with the word JESUS.

J—Joy
E—Everlasting
S—Supreme
U—Unity
S—Saves

Have family members share their acrostics. Discuss the various words that are selected.

Read and Explain. Have a family member read and explain a Scripture passage.

Read and Comment. Have a family member read a Scripture verse. Then go around the family circle with each person commenting on what he feels the verse means, on what he likes about it or on an experience he has had in applying that verse to life.

Sermon Search. We have had many good times with this activity. Sermon Search starts at church and is completed at home. The following seven activities are for your family to do during the sermon. Assign two of these on a Sunday morning. After lunch (or at some other appropriate time) have your family share their completed activities and discuss the message.

1. Illustrate the sermon.
2. What was the main point?

3. What part of the sermon did I like best?
4. The sermon made me feel_____.
5. I didn't understand_____.
6. As a Christian I should_____ .
7. Prepare a quiz. Have each person prepare two questions about the sermon. Collect the questions and take the test. Who listened closest to the sermon?

News Item. Clip out interesting news items and talk about them at the dinner table. There are many types of news items. Some show the world's need for Christ. Others show how God's love is put into practice. Still others are just interesting happenings. You might want to have one of your children select what he feels is the "news item of the week" and talk about it at the dinner hour. Whenever possible, use news items as a springboard for discussing scriptural principles.

Discuss Debate. You can have some lively times with this activity. Select a discussion topic, such as: "Are most Christians hypocrites?" "Should a Christian ever tell a lie?" "Does God always answer our prayers the way we want Him to?" "Is an occasional drink of alcohol okay?"

Tell family members that you will start this discussion and sometime during the discussion you will stop them and choose two persons to take opposite views and debate the issue for two minutes.

After the debate continue the discussion.

Last Letter Add a Word. One family member starts this activity by saying a Bible word such as "John." The person on his left must say another Bible word starting with the last letter of the word just given. For example, he might say "Noah," because Noah starts with *N,* the last letter of John. See how many times you can go around the family circle with each person adding a word.

Who Am I? Have someone think of a Bible character and say, "Who am I?" Other members of the family, in turn, ask questions about his identity which can be answered yes or no. The person who correctly identifies the Bible character is the winner and is next to ask, "Who am I?"

Read Together. Select a book and read a chapter or two. Continue reading each evening until the book is finished.

Card Clues. About once a week hide a card clue under a family member's plate. No one is allowed to look under his plate until the meal is over and Mom or Dad gives the signal. The person who discovers the card clue must read it aloud and follow the instructions.

Write the following instructions on index cards or make up clues of your own:

- Tell a funny story.
- Play follow the leader. The family must copy you for the next five minutes.
- You may ask a favor of Dad.
- Check under your beds for a surprise.
- Say something nice about the person on your right.
- Quote or read your favorite Scripture verse.
- Lead a song.
- Ask Mother a Bible question.
- Select a family member to sing a solo.
- Surprise! We are going out for ice cream cones.
- Pantomime an Old Testament story.
- Pantomime a New Testament story.
- Play "Who am I?"—You are it.
- Tell the funniest thing that happened to you this week.
- Tell a joke.
- Lead a discussion on why Judas betrayed Christ.

- Lead a discussion on why one thief on the cross trusted Jesus and the other didn't.
- Have everyone think of a number between 1 and 15. The person who comes closest must do a chore for you.
- Congratulations! You have just won the Helper Award. During the next week you must do one helpful thing for each family member.
- Tell when you feel closest to God.

Problem-Solution. This activity encourages family members to help one another with their problems. One family member tells the person on his left a personal problem. He might say, for example, "I'm having trouble with math at school and the teacher doesn't seem to care." The person on the left then shares a possible solution to that problem, perhaps, "Why don't you ask your teacher for an appointment and then ask him for some suggestions on how you can improve?"

Continue around the table until each person states a problem and helps another with a solution.

Change the Subject. For this activity you will need a medium-sized ball. After dinner seat the family in a circle on the floor. Explain to your family that you will start talking about an interesting subject and at any moment during your conversation you may roll the ball to another family member. That person must start talking about a new subject of his own. When he wishes, that person may roll the ball to another family member and that person must start a new subject. Continue the game until everyone has participated.

Ties that Bind Us

"Suppertime . . . that final meal when the day was

almost over. The tradition of the family table. In letting it slip away from us I'm afraid we've lost something precious. We've cheated our children, stunted their social growth, gagged their articulation, cut off too early those ties that nature meant for us. The ties that bind us to people in the same family, people who represent comfort, security, nourishment, not only of body but of spirit. Ties that used to be gathered up at the close of day and drawn together, if not always in peace, at least in fellowship and caring. . . .

"I wish that by some magic I could step to the door and hear it echoing from every house for blocks. *'Suppertime! Come on in, supper's ready!'* "[9]

Our family enthusiastically agrees! We feel that those "ties that bind us" can be strengthened through good times at the dinner hour.

Footnotes

1. Marjorie Holmes, *You and I and Yesterday* (New York: Bantam Books, 1974), p. 148.
2. "Family Eating Study Yields Food for Thought," *Today's Child*, vol. 22 (March, 1974), p. 1.
3. "Family Eating Study . . ." p. 1.
4. James H. S. Bossard, "Family Table Talk—An Area for Sociological Study," in *Neglected Areas in Family Living*, Thomas E. Sullinger (North Quincy, Mass.: Christopher Publishing House, 1960), pp. 121, 122.
5. Paul White, "Jungle Doctor" series (Chicago: Moody Press).
6. Dorothy Johnston, "Pete and Penny" series (Chicago: Moody Press).
7. Laura Ingalls Wilder, "Little House Books" series (New York: Harper and Row, Publishers, Inc.).
8. Gladys Hunt, *Honey for a Child's Heart* (Grand Rapids: Zondervan Publishing House, 1969).
9. Holmes, *You and I and Yesterday*, pp. 156, 157.

8

Developing a
Creative Family
Bible Study

"What about a verse by verse study of the Bible?" people ask. "Is there an interesting way in which our family can study a theme, book or section of Scripture?"

I believe those of you who are asking this question will find what I call Creative Family Bible Study an enjoyable and exciting way to share the Scriptures at home.

One feature that makes Creative Family Bible Study unique is that the leadership is shared. A different family member leads each week, or however often you decide to meet. Each family member prepares for the Bible study and shares his ideas with the rest of the family.

How often you have a family Bible study is up to you. At the end of this chapter I give a variety of ways in which these family times can be scheduled. Use one of these or design a schedule of your own.

How to Start a Family Bible Study

The following is a simple five-step plan that will help you start a Creative Family Bible Study in your home.

Step 1: Bible Study Material

Choose what Bible material you would like to study, such as a whole book (James, Mark or Acts, for example), a Scripture portion (such as the Sermon on the Mount or Col. 3) or a topic (such as grace, sin, death, etc.). Divide the material into short, easy-to-cover sections for your Bible study. (See the example on page 72.)

Step 2: Bible Study Notebook

Give each family member a Bible study notebook. (Loose-leaf works best but spiral or other kinds are adequate.) The 13 Activities for Preparing a Family Bible Study listed on page 70 should be written on the first page of each person's notebook.

Step 3: Bible Study Leadership

Explain to your family that leadership will be a shared responsibility. Each person, in his turn, will lead a Bible study. The leader for the *following* session is to come to the current Bible study prepared to assign family members two preparation activities (see Activities for Preparing a Family Bible Study in this chapter) for the next Bible study.

Step 4: Bible Study Preparation

Each person is to prepare for the Bible study by completing the two assigned activities. Some families might want to use the Family Bible Study Prepare and Share Worksheet (shown on page 71) to help guide individual preparation and family Bible study.

Step 5: Bible Study Sharing

The leader should guide the discussion and encourage

everyone to participate in an open, loving way. Every family member should share his two activities and any insights he gained from his study. At the end of each Bible study, if appropriate, have each person write one thing he will do during the week to "live out" the Scripture that has been studied. Close with prayer.

Tools for Preparing a Family Bible Study

At the start of a new study series it would be helpful to look at the background of the Bible book or section you have decided to study. An interesting way to do this is to assign each member one of the following questions to answer on your first Bible study of the new series:

The Writer: Who was he?
Why did he write?
The Readers: Who were they?
What was their world like?

Answers to these questions and similar ones can be found in standard Bible study tools: Bible dictionary, concordance, Bible atlas, commentary or a Bible handbook. These books, together with several translations of the Bible, will help your Bible study immensely.

Activities for Preparing a Family Bible Study

Your family might want to use the Prepare and Share Worksheet to help organize your family Bible study. The list of 13 activities can help family members *prepare* for Bible study. Two of these activities are to be assigned by the person who is to lead the next Bible study. The leader should carefully read the Scripture portion to be studied and choose the two activities he feels will be most helpful to family members as they prepare for the Bible study.

Each person does his assignment on the "prepare"

portion and the "share" section is used during the Bible study.

Activities

1. Give a brief summary of this Scripture.

2. What do you feel was the most important thought or verse?

3. What part of the Scripture do you like best?

4. Does this Scripture point out a weakness in your life that needs to be strengthened? What one thing can you do to strengthen that weakness?

5. What does this Scripture say an ideal Christian should or should not do?

6. Write two questions about this Scripture.

7. List the words or thoughts you did not understand.

8. Paraphrase the Scripture.

9. Illustrate the Scripture. (Draw a picture.)

10. Memorize a key verse. (Leader should assign the verse.)

11. How could this Scripture help our home be a happier place to live?

12. Use a Bible dictionary or commentary to define the following words _____. (The leader chooses the words to be defined.)

13. Be prepared to ask and answer a question about the Scripture. (Here's the way this activity works. On Bible study night, first read the passage aloud. Next, each person asks and answers a question. One family member starts the activity by asking the person on his left a question about the Scripture passage. The person answers and then asks the person on his left a question. Continue this procedure until each family member asks and answers a question.)

Family Bible Study
Prepare and Share Worksheet
(example)

P Scripture_____
R Assignment_____

R Activity 1_____
E _____
P _____
A _____
_____

A Activity 2_____
R _____
E _____
_____
_____

and

S Insights from our sharing_____
H _____
A _____

A What I will do to "live out" this Scripture
R during the week_____
E _____
_____

Prayer list_____
_____
_____
_____

Scheduling Your Family Bible Study

An appealing feature of Creative Family Bible Study is that it is a simple approach to sharing Bible truth together. Each person spends about 15 minutes in preparation. The Bible study itself lasts approximately 30 to 45 minutes.

I suggest you try Creative Family Bible Study and see how your family responds. Matthew 7:1-5 would be a good section of Scripture to study. Decide as a family if you would like to continue this approach to Bible study. Next select how often you would like to meet.

Some families will want to meet weekly. A book of the Bible such as James or a large section of Scripture such as the Sermon on the Mount (Matt. 5—7) works well for the weekly schedule. The book of James, divided into easy-to-study sections would take four months to complete on a weekly schedule. The divisions may be as follows: James 1:1-4; 5-8; 9-11; 12-18; 19-27; 2:1-7; 8-13; 14-26; 3:1-12; 13-18; 4:1-10; 11; 12; 13-17; 5:1-6; 7-12; 13-19.

A once-a-month schedule might appeal to some families. In such cases a shorter section of Scripture is best; for example, Colossians 3. This passage might be divided in the following way: Colossians 3:1-4; 5-11; 12-17; 18-25.

Family vacations provide a good opportunity to spend time sharing God's Word together. Select a portion of Scripture or a topic you would like to study while on vacation and set aside some time for Creative Family Bible Study.

Adapt Creative Family Bible Study to meet the needs and time schedule of your family. Remember the important thing is that you have a consistent plan for Bible sharing in your family.

9

Memorizing
Scripture
Together

A few months ago our vivacious five-year-old Bridget seemed to be competing with the first-grade boy next door for the title Worst Behaved Child on the Block!

Janet and I discussed the situation and decided one of the problems was that we had been spoiling our "baby." We committed ourselves to a more firm and consistent plan of discipline with Bridget.

During the next couple of days that firmness was vigorously carried out in various ways, including some applications to the back of Bridget's lap. After the second day of our new approach with Bridget I met her in her room for a little discussion.

I asked, "Bridget, do you know that in the Bible God says He wants you to obey your parents?" Bridget looked at me in disbelief and answered, "No, He doesn't."

I picked up her *Living Bible,* opened it to Ephesians 6:1 and read, "Children, obey your parents; this is the right thing to do because God has placed them in authority over you."

We talked about the verse for a few minutes and then I asked Bridget to find a picture in a magazine that would remind her of the verse. Soon she had cut out an appropriate picture.

I wanted her to memorize the verse, so I had her repeat it after me several times until she had it perfect. "Now Bridget," I asked, "will you try very hard to do what this verse says?" She quickly nodded her head. By this time she was open to anything that would ease the pressure at home.

That afternoon her friend, the little six-year-old boy from next door, came to see Bridget. She met him and said, "John, come on to my room. I have something to show you." I quietly followed them to see what was going to happen.

Bridget picked up the picture she cut out of the magazine and handed it to John. "Here," she said, "you need to look at this too. Obey your parents; this is the right thing to do."

That verse stayed with Bridget, although she doesn't always apply it perfectly. But we have seen some positive changes in her behavior.

Memorizing Scripture together can be a very valuable family activity. When we understand, memorize and use key Scriptures, they become an integral part of our thinking process. God's Word internalized can help us become mature persons in Christ, the goal of every Christian.

The Scripture Memory Rule

The following four principles will be a helpful tool for your family memory times. We will call this series of principles the RULE for family memorization. Our rule is expressed in four key words, the first letters of which spell RULE:

> **R**—Reason
> **U**—Understand
> **L**—Learn
> **E**—Execute

We will look at each principle and see how it can help us make our family memory times enjoyable character-building experiences.

Step 1: Reason

Bridget was highly motivated to memorize Ephesians 6:1. Why? Because her behavior had her in big trouble. She had a reason to memorize that verse. It was going to help her.

For your family to memorize Scripture together and for God's Word to have a genuine impact on their lives, they must have a valid reason for memorizing it. This is especially true with children. They must see how their effort will be useful.

There are some general reasons why Christians should memorize Scripture. Share these with your family. Psalm 1 exalts the person whose "delight is in the law of the Lord; and in his law doth he meditate day and night" (Ps. 1:2). This person's life, the psalm says, will be happy and prosperous.

Psalm 119:11 gives another reason for memorizing

Scripture: "Thy word have I hid in mine heart, that I might not sin against thee." Jesus gives us a beautiful example of the application of this verse in the record of His temptation in the wilderness (Matt. 4:1-11). Jesus was able to answer Satan's temptations by quoting God's Word which He "hid" in His heart.

Second Timothy 3:16,17 answers the question why memorize Scripture? in another way. I like J.B. Phillips' paraphrase of these verses: "All scripture is inspired by God and is useful for teaching the faith and correcting error, for re-setting the direction of a man's life and training him in good living. The scriptures are the comprehensive equipment of the man of God, and fit him fully for all branches of his work."

Since Scripture is the "comprehensive equipment of the man of God," and can train us for "good living," it seems to me that a thorough knowledge of God's Word, including memorization, should be a high priority in a Christian family.

Commit yourselves to these general reasons for memorizing Scripture. Then each time your family decides to memorize a verse or passage discuss the specific reasons why that particular verse or passage is helpful. How can it be useful in our individual lives? In our family?

Step 2: Understand

In discussing why you should memorize a certain verse your family will begin to understand the meaning of that verse. But go beyond that to a deeper analysis of its meaning until each family member has a good grasp of the content.

Ephesians 6:1 was easy for Bridget to memorize because she understood what it meant. Her understanding was deepened when she found a picture that helped her visualize the verse.

There are a variety of ways in which you can help your family understand the verse you want to memorize. Discussion can be stimulated by selecting one of the following activities:

Paraphrase. This is a good way to see if a person really understands what the verse says. Have each family member rewrite the verse using his own words. Read your paraphrases aloud and discuss the differences.

Most Important Word. Have family members choose what they feel is the most important word in the verse and share it with the rest of the family.

Read and Explain. Have each person read the Scripture to himself and then explain what he feels the verse means.

A Word I Do Not Understand. Have each person write down one word they don't understand. Discuss these words. Use a Bible dictionary or commentary if necessary.

Know-Feel-Do. Have each person write down what they think the verse says a Christian should know, feel and do. Share and discuss your thoughts with one another. Personalize "do." What does this verse say *I* should do?

Illustrate the Verse. Let each person illustrate the verse by drawing a picture or symbol based on his understanding of the verse. Another option is to have family members find a picture in a magazine that reminds them of the verse, cut it out and paste it on a piece of paper. Have them explain why they selected that picture.

Pantomime. Have each person pantomime (act out silently) the verse or verses.

Step 3: Learn

With a good knowledge of what the verse means you are ready to learn or memorize it. There are two steps to this: repeat and recall.

Repeat. Repeat the verse you wish to memorize a section at a time. For example, if you choose to memorize Ephesians 4:26 you could divide it as follows: If you are angry/don't sin by nursing your grudge/get over it quickly (*TLB*).

Repeat a section several times together and then add another section until the whole family can say the entire verse.

Recall. When each person has memorized the verse, select an interesting way for family members to recall it. Here are several methods you might want to use:

1. Add a word. Say the first word of the verse and go around the family circle, having each person add a word until the Scripture is completed. If someone misses a word start the verse over. Continue until you can go around without missing a word.

2. Mixed up Scripture Verse. Write each word of the verse on a 3x5 index card. Shuffle the cards and lay them out on a table or on the floor. Have the family put them in order. You might want to time yourselves and see how fast the verse can be put in order.

3. Recite. Have each person, in turn, recite the complete verse.

4. Card Game. Larry Richards, in his helpful booklet *Helping My Child Memorize Scripture,* gives an interesting recall game:

"Another variation of the game theme is to print the words of a number of verses or verse phrases on 3x5 cards. These cards are then shuffled and stacked in the middle of the table. Each player turns over a word card, and either keeps or discards it. The object is to collect all the words in a particular verse or part of a verse. The first one to lay down a completed verse or phrase wins. If all the cards are picked up by players without having a winner, players can trade word cards without showing the word or words they are trading, until one completes his verse."[1]

Step 4: Execute

God's Word is practical. It is to train us for good living (2 Tim. 3:16, *Phillips*). We are to execute, or put into action, God's instructions. This is a vital and exciting part of memorizing God's Word.

For Bridget this meant obeying her parents. Janet and I were able to say to her, "Bridget, we are very proud of the way you have been obeying us. You are doing what your memory verse says."

Bridget felt some genuine accomplishment from putting God's Word into action. This is where genuine Christian growth occurs, not just from hearing and knowing but from doing, cooperating with God to make changes in our lives.

Plan some projects to help family members put the memorized verse into action. You might have each person write one way in which he will seek to live out the verse during the week. Have a report session the following week.

Another way to encourage family members to apply Scripture to their lives is to have each person start a Scripture memorization diary. Write down each verse that has been memorized and a brief account of each time it was put into practice as shown on page 80.

VERSE	ACTION
"And now this word to all of you.	Today Marsha called me a name and I got very angry. I prayed for her tonight and asked God to forgive my anger.
"You should be like one big happy family full of sympathy toward each other, loving one another with tender hearts and humble minds.	
"Don't repay evil for evil. Don't snap back at those who say unkind things about you. Instead, pray for God's help for them for we are to be kind to others, and God will bless us for it" (1 Pet. 3:8,9 *TLB*).	Today I showed sympathy to Mom because I knew she wasn't feeling well. I picked up the house without being asked.

We have now gone through the RULE of memorization: Reason, Understand, Learn, and Execute. The next question is, how do we get started as a family?

Memorizing Scripture on Family Night

We suggest you start by having a special Family Night or a family time devoted to the subject of Scripture memorization. Feel free to adapt the following family time plan to fit the needs and interests of your family.

Start your family time by explaining that the purpose of this time together is to discuss the importance of memorizing God's Word. Then choose some of the following projects to do as a family:

Our Secret Bible. Explain that years ago it was against the law to own a Bible. In fact, it still is in some countries. People are arrested, sometimes even killed for owning one. Discuss: How do you think Christians feel without a Bible? How would you feel? What would you do? Do you feel it is possible that some day owning a Bible could be against the law in our country? Explain that you are going to pretend it is against the law to own a Bible in America and all the Bibles have been burned. Now, in the secret of your home you are going to make your own family Bible from verses you can remember. Have each member write down all the verses or parts of verses he can remember. Do this by lantern or candlelight for added effect. After an appropriate amount of time have family members share their verses. Fill in the gaps. Work together to make all the verses and passages as accurate as possible. Appoint a scribe to take all the Scriptures and put them in booklet form. Suggest that he have it ready for the next Family Night.

Discuss what you have done. How big is your secret Bible? Are you satisfied with the verses you know? How big would your family Bible be if each person had memorized regularly since becoming a Christian? Do you feel it would be helpful for the family to memorize Scripture together on a regular basis?

Why Should We Memorize? Discuss further some reasons why a Christian should memorize Scripture. Each person will need a Bible, a pencil and paper. Assign each of the following Scripture passages to a different family member: 2 Tim. 3:16,17; Pss. 1:2; 119:11; Matt. 4:1-11. While the verses are read aloud have each person make a list of reasons why it is important to memorize Scripture. These reasons should be based on the Scriptures just read. Have each person read his list. Decide as a family which reasons are most important and write these on a large sheet of paper.

Roleplay. If you have younger children, they will enjoy acting out the story of Jesus' temptation by the devil. Read the story first (Matt. 4:1-11) and then act it out. Discuss: What did Jesus do when He was tempted? Why was He able to quote a Scripture each time He was tempted? Is it important for us to memorize Scripture? Why?

Memorize a Verse. Now would be a good time to memorize a verse together. Use Ephesians 4:26 or select a verse of your own. Follow the RULE of memorization. First have someone in the family read the verse aloud. Next have each member give one *reason* why he feels this verse would be helpful to memorize. How might it be used?

1. *Now make sure everyone understands the verse.* You may use one of the six activities for understanding, or design your own.

2. *Learn the verse together.* Repeat the verse together a section at a time until you can say the whole verse. When the family has memorized the verse, select one of the five interesting ways to help the family recall the verse.

3. *Help family members apply the verse to their lives.* This is the critical part—the execution or application. If you have chosen to memorize Ephesians 4:26, here's a project you can do. This verse says, "If you are angry, don't let the sun go down with you still angry—get over it quickly."

Give each person a piece of paper. Have him write the verse on it. Now have everyone make three columns, as shown in the example on the next page:

Why did I become angry?	What did I do about my anger?	Draw a smiley face if you did not go to bed angry.

Explain that each time a person becomes angry during the next week he should write something in the appropriate columns. At your next Family Time have individuals share their lists with one another. This would also be a good time to talk about anger: what the Bible has to say about it, its causes, how to express it in legitimate ways.

A Challenge

I would like to challenge your family to do a project during the next year. How about memorizing one verse a month together? Some families might want to do more, but for many one verse would be a good start. Here is a list of verses you may begin with: Philippians 2:4; James 1:19; Ephesians 4:15; Proverbs 15:1; Ephesians 4:32; Proverbs 17:14; 1 Thessalonians 5:11,15; Galatians 6:2; Proverbs 16:28; 1 John 3:18; 1 Peter 3:8.

Footnote

1. Lawrence Richards, *Helping My Child Memorize Scripture* (Cincinnati: Standard Publishing, 1975), pp. 13,14.

10

Teaching in Informal Moments

Have you ever experienced a family tragedy? Our family has. A while ago an immediate member of our family, Miss Rascal Jean Rickerson, died suddenly and unexpectedly. Rascal was a cute little one-year-old golden hamster that belonged to our oldest daughter.

Heidi was heartbroken over the death of Rascal but quickly recuperated to make the final arrangements for her burial. She asked me to be the all-purpose funeral director. I was to put Rascal in her casket, dig the grave and officiate at the funeral. The entire family gathered in the backyard for the graveside service. We buried Rascal in her final resting place and decorated the grave.

Each family member took a few moments to thank God for pets and for the opportunity we had to love Rascal for a whole year. I never saw our girls pray so earnestly, although I suspect they were secretly praying for a sudden resurrection. For a brief moment my wife and I stepped into our children's world to share with them the truth that their heavenly Father loves children so much that He created animals that can be enjoyed as pets.

We used this common occurrence, the death of a pet, to teach of God's love. The teaching was spontaneous and informal. Just a simple thought. Our children, however, will never forget that lesson. Why? Because we were focusing on a topic of great interest and concern to them. This was a true life situation. Rascal was dead, and that really hurt.

Many of life's lessons are best taught in this way. In Deuteronomy 6 God, speaking through Moses, stressed the importance of informal teaching. The Israelite parents were told to model God's laws (teaching by example), to teach them diligently to their children (formal teaching) and to talk of them continually (informal teaching). Deuteronomy 6:7 says, "And thou shalt . . . talk of them when thou sittest in thine house, and when thou walkest by the way, and when thou liest down, and when thou risest up." In other words they were to teach from life itself—informally in everyday situations.

Teaching in the Present Tense

This type of teaching makes sense to children. Much of what they are required to learn does not. Children often hear, "This will help you someday." Someday means nothing to a child who is involved only in his immediate world. He really doesn't care about "someday"; he cares about *now*. This does not mean, of course, that we should drop all teaching that will be mainly useful in the future. It means, however, that we should teach Christian values by sharing those Scripture insights that will help them *now.*

Janet and I recently shared with our girls a verse of Scripture that they were able to use immediately. Heidi and Liesl were to begin at a new school. They had some real fears about this adventure. Monday morning, before they started out for their first day at the new school, Janet and I sat down with Heidi and Liesl and discussed their feelings about attending there. We shared with them Philippians 4:6, which says, "Be careful [anxious] for nothing, but in everything by prayer and supplication with thanksgiving let your requests be made known to God."

The girls became visibly more relaxed as they realized God would help them adjust to the new school. We spent a few minutes in prayer, each person asking God to give confidence to Liesl and Heidi.

The girls learned two important lessons. They learned that God is even interested in the funny feeling little girls get in their stomachs when they are about to start a new school. They also learned that God's Word is practical. It can help nine- and ten-year-old girls face their problems—now!

Teaching from Heart to Heart

Deuteronomy 6:4-6 tells us what the source of informal teaching is to be. "Hear, O Israel: The Lord our God is one Lord: And thou shalt love the Lord thy God with all thine heart, and with all thy soul, and with all thy might. And these words, which I command thee this day, shall be in thine heart."

Notice that our own relationship with God comes first. The love of God is to be in our own hearts, His Word

86

deeply internalized in our own lives. *Then* we are to talk of these things to our children (see Deut. 6:7). This is the nature of informal teaching—heart to heart, life to life.

When we are conscious of what God is doing in our own lives, then we are able to help our children see how God is working in their lives. They need to see evidence of our belief that God is involved and interested in everything they do. When they see us depend on God and give Him the glory for all things, they will learn to do the same.

We should also talk to our children about how God is working in our lives. If God is helping us overcome fear or anger, we should discuss it with our children. If God is helping the family overcome a financial crisis, we should share it with them. It is good when we tell our children about our victories and successes, emphasizing that they are all for the glory of God.

Teaching from Weakness

We recently went through a family crisis that strengthened each person's faith in God. We were to enter into a new ministry at the start of the school year. We had known about the move for eight months, and yet nothing seemed to be going right for us. Our house had not sold, and twice we had seen deals on possible new houses fall through. Now, two weeks before school was to start, we were desperately trying to find a place to rent. Nothing suitable was available. We were terribly discouraged. Where had we gone wrong? We really trusted the Lord to lead us in the sale of our house and the purchase of another one. Why wasn't God answering our prayers? Maybe this new ministry wasn't of the Lord.

I'll never forget a certain night when my wife and I sat

down for our together time. I remember thinking, "Boy, this is going to be great. I don't even feel like praying." I can remember my prayer very clearly. It was short and to the point. "God I'm terribly discouraged. I don't understand all this. But I do know that you promised I'll never be tested beyond a point that I can endure. I kind of feel I'm at that point, Lord. Please help."

As my wife and I checked on the girls before going to bed that night, I noticed that our oldest girl was crying. "What's wrong Heidi?" I asked.

"Dad, I'm really discouraged about this house thing. What's going to happen?"

"I don't know Heidi," I answered. "I'm really down myself. I don't have any more answers than you have. I only know that God said He will answer our prayers, and we have trusted that He knows what is best for us."

Not very consoling words for an 11-year-old girl, was it? But Janet and I determined we were not going to sweep things under the rug for fear of making our children feel insecure. We believed they needed to see us in our spiritual struggle.

Our miracle happened the next day. As I walked into the house from work Janet said, "Wayne, long distance from Rich LaFarge. They think they found a house we will like."

Here it was. The answer we were waiting for. A house in the exact area we wanted, available when we wanted it. What a lesson. God taught us, once again, that our timing is not His timing, and that indeed He will not let us be tested beyond the point of our endurance.

What a family celebration we had at the local ice cream parlor. We talked about this miracle in our life. We talked about how discouraged we were. We discussed the fact that God never lets us down and how He always knows what's best for us. We praised God for His goodness.

If Janet and I had hidden our doubts and fears from the children, they could not feel the impact of this great informal learning experience. This teaching was heart to heart, life to life. It involved both the despair and the joy that are parts of every Christian life. We thank God for this lesson He taught us and the opportunity to "talk" of it with our children.

Sharpening Our Focus

We can sharpen our focus in our informal teaching by concentrating on the following areas:

Be Aware of What God Is Doing in Your Life. I have already mentioned this but I can't emphasize it enough. Informal teaching is life to life. You cannot share if you have nothing to give.

Involve Yourself in Your Child's Life. This is a critical area of all the teaching you do. Teaching depends, above all else, on relationship. The feelings that have developed between you and your child will determine whether or not he will be open to your teaching.

The best way to develop a loving relationship is to show your child that you are interested in everything he does. Talk with him. Ask questions. Listen. Have special times when you are alone with each child. Plan recreational times together. Don't expect your child to be excited about the things you feel are important if you show little interest in his world. A child's world is a world of play, and excellent relationships can be built as parents play with their children.

Look for Opportunities. Every day we have many

opportunities for informal teaching with our children. We need to sharpen our spiritual vision so that we will take advantage of more natural opportunities. I would like to mention several areas in particular that lend themselves to informal teaching:

Nature. Our world is a book on God's greatness and love. During a hike through the woods we can talk about flowers, trees, birds, animals, insects—all things God has created. On one camping trip I woke the children up late at night and carried them outside the cabin to observe a sky glittering with stars. I talked with them about the beauty and vastness of the universe.

Last summer we stood together in the magnificent mountains of Snoqualmi Pass in the state of Washington. The whole family was overwhelmed with the majesty of those mountains and alpine meadows. Janet remembered Psalm 121:1, which says, "I will lift up mine eyes unto the hills, from whence cometh my help." We all felt that divine help and strength in a moment of worship. Then we shared our feelings with one another.

Problems. One of the major tasks children have is learning to get along with other people. Many of the problems our children bring to us or that we observe within the home are of that nature. Such relationship problems are beautiful teaching opportunities for us, because that is what the Bible is all about—loving God and loving our brother as ourselves.

We can share with our children some of the key Scriptures that can teach them better ways of relating with others. Various passages show how to make allowances for differences (Phil. 2:1-4; Eph. 4:2); encourage kindness and forgiveness (Eph. 4:32); give guidance toward better communication (Jas. 1:19); teach new ways

90

of responding to others (Prov. 15:1); show how to channel and express anger (Prov. 14:29; Eph. 4:26); give direction on speaking the truth in love (Eph. 4:15). And, of course, the Bible offers many other helps on improving our relationship with one another.

The verses we share with our children should first be part of our lives. We should memorize them and live them out. Then when our children notice that we are relating to others in a Christlike way, they will be able to transfer these same principles to their lives.

Whatever problems our children might be facing, there is always a scriptural principle to be applied. However, the ideal is not that we give them ready-made answers to the difficult situations they face. It is rather that we equip them to work through the problems themselves. When we respond with pat answers, we hinder their growth as persons. Our task as parents is to give them a biblical framework within which they can creatively work out their own solutions.

Contrast in Life-styles. The Christian and the non-Christian live in vastly different worlds. Our children remind us of that as they bring home stories of the value systems of other families. The other day Liesl said, "Dad, you ought to see all the stuff Sharon has. Would you believe that each person in her family has his own ten-speed bike and TV set? They're lucky."

I saw my opportunity. "Liesl," I replied, "is there something important that Sharon doesn't have?"

"Yeah, she doesn't have a Dad. Her Mom and Dad are separated." That initiated an interesting discussion between Liesl and me on what really is important in a family and what happens sometimes when families place great importance on material things.

Questions. Children are naturally inquisitive. We need to encourage this, because questions our children ask can be great informal teaching opportunities. "Dad, why did Jesus have to die?" "Mom, is it true that even people who haven't heard of Jesus will go to hell?"

How would you answer these questions? One way to stimulate discussion is to turn the question back to the person who asked it and to the rest of the family. "Why do *you* think Jesus had to die?" "What do *you* think will happen to the people who have not heard of Jesus?" After an appropriate amount of discussion, get out your Bible concordance and have the family look together to see what God's Word has to say about the question. Certainly, as a parent you need to give your input, but remember sermons and authoritarian statements tend to bring discussion and thinking to a halt. A healthy, even lively, family discussion will accomplish more than a pat answer.

Dinner and Bedtime Opportunities. I have already devoted a chapter to dinnertime teaching, but let me add this. In addition to any planned teaching you might do, look for the informal opportunities. In many homes most of the talk and fellowship is unplanned and unstructured. I know this is true in ours. Offhand comments by your children can be turned into lively discussion and genuine learning opportunities for the entire family.

Bedtime also offers good informal teaching opportunities. I realize there are also some limitations at this time of night. Often we are at the end of our patience with the kids. We're anxious to get them out of the way, and fast! They may have already used every trick in the book to stay up.

But there are nevertheless many opportunities for deep

personal sharing at this time of the day. Genuine problems seem to surface as children lie in the quiet of their rooms. We can certainly think of rich experiences that have grown out of childish sharing of bedtime anxieties and fears. We need to be sensitive to such moments. Some of our best informal teaching can be done at bedtime.

Informal teaching can be exciting as we watch God open up opportunities for us to share with our children. May I challenge you to another goal? During the next month keep a record of each time you are able to share informally with your children. You might want to set up your record on a piece of paper as shown in the illustration below:

Date:	The situation was:	I responded by:

You will be amazed at how often you are involved in teaching your children through everyday occurrences.

11

Using Recreation to Build the Family

If you were to ask your children, "What is your best family memory?" what do you think their answer would be? During one dinner conversation I asked our children that question, and I was not surprised by their answers. Liesl said, "Bible Rock, Dad. The camping trip at Bible Rock is my best memory." Heidi voted for our vacations on the beach at Lincoln City, Oregon. Bridget said, "My best memory is running on the sand dunes."

I had expected the children's answers would be about family recreation. I suspect your children's responses would be similar. To children, times of family recreation are important and they recall them quickly as the best memories of all.

A Leisure Atmosphere for Informal Teaching

But why? What is there about a family playing together that is so important to children? That night as we sat around our dinner table we discussed this.

Bridget and Liesl both felt that "doing things together" is what makes family recreation so important. Liesl said, "Dad, I think we get to know one another better when we play together." Heidi really put her finger on a crucial element of family recreation. She said, "I feel more open when you and Mom are doing things with us *that we like to do."*

Heidi's insight was sound. Playing with children does create openness, or as Marion Leach Jacobsen says, "a closeness that is very tangible."[1]

The business of being an adult erects walls between parents and children. Let's face it, we do live in a different world than our children do. But as Heidi implies, all that changes when we play together. Through recreation we enter our children's world of play. As we step into their world through the door of family recreation we are telling our children, "We really care because we are taking time to do what you feel is important."

Recreation times together contribute to the openness that is so important to building a loving relationship with our children. Without it our teaching will be ineffective.

I see family recreation as a living out of Philippians 2:4, which says, "Do not merely look out for your own personal interests, but also for the interests of others" (*NASB*). When we play with our children we zero in on their interests. We model for them the fact that Christian love expresses itself in concrete ways. By showing our interest in them we teach our children in a very visible way that they should be sensitive to the "interests of others." They also learn to be concerned with us and with what we as their parents feel is important for them.

All three principles of teaching Christian values given in Deuteronomy 6—*model, teach, talk* (see chapter 4)—

can be used during family recreation. We have already mentioned how we *model* love and sensitivity to the interests of others.

There are times when you can *teach* a special devotional thought or Scripture in connection with what you are doing. For example on a trip to the lake you might take a few minutes to discuss Jesus walking on the water or stilling the storm.

The family closeness developed through recreation creates an atmosphere in which our *talk* (the informal teaching of Deuteronomy 6) is very natural.

You can use this closeness to open up family sharing, but you must be the model by which your children learn to share. Work toward talking about Jesus and your walk with Him as naturally as you talk about your best friend and your favorite sport. Encourage spontaneous sharing by sharing your own thoughts with your children.

Plan for Family Recreation

I believe it is vital to plan for family recreation. My wife and I plan family recreation during our weekly together times. We write our leisure plans on calendar. When we fail to do so, the quality of Rickerson family recreation is much poorer. I believe a family should plan some type of recreational activity to do together each week. It doesn't have to be elaborate or expensive. Simple things like a bike ride, a walk, playing a table game, or reading together can be very enjoyable. Check out with your family what they would like to do. Janet and I plan activities based on total input. We find out each family member's interests and base our decisions on what is best for the entire family.

I suggest you have a family time specifically to plan for

family recreation. The best ideas for family recreation will come from your family, not from books. Have a family brainbust. Have family members suggest as many recreation ideas as possible, while one person writes them on a sheet of paper. After you have a large number of ideas, vote as a family on the "top ten." Then get out the calendar and schedule these activities.

You'll be surprised by the many good suggestions for family recreation your family will come up with. If you want additional ideas, your library has books to help you. We have already mentioned Marion Leach Jacobsen's book, *How to Keep Your Family Together . . . and Still Have Fun*, which has many ideas on family recreation. *Heaven Help the Home*, by Howard Hendricks, also has a good chapter on things to do as a family.[2]

Family recreation is an important part of teaching Christian values in the family. These times together will provide our children with some of their fondest memories. Our responsibility as parents is to carefully plan opportunities for our children to build such life-long memories.

> Happy thoughts
> Of good times past
> Make memories
> That last and last.[3]

Footnotes

1. Marion Leach Jacobsen, *How to Keep Your Family Together . . . and Still Have Fun* (Grand Rapids: Zondervan Publishing House, 1972), p. 14.
2. Howard G. Hendricks, *Heaven Help the Home!* (New York: Berkley Publishing Corp., 1975).
3. Source unknown.

12

Especially for Church Leaders

Many churches want to get entire families together for a time of learning and fellowship but don't know how to go about it.

At Beaverton Christian Church we have Family Enabling Nights. On the last Monday night of the month families with children from babies through teenage arrive at church at 7:00 P.M. for a time of sharing.

We start the evening by grouping three to five families together in family clusters. We then give them an activity to do together that takes about 20 minutes.

After the family cluster activity the children see a movie or have recreation while the parents meet for specific training we call Parent Enabling. This one-hour session is broken into sharing, input and planning.

To conclude the evening families come back together for a time of fellowship over delicious desserts. (Each family brings a dessert. That's enough to make any evening a success!)

Our families are very enthusiastic about these evenings, which tells me that families really do like to learn and fellowship together with other families regardless of the spread in ages.

How to Organize a Family Enabling Night

Step 1: Family Cluster

The evening starts with three to five families joining together in a family activity for about 20 minutes. It is best to group families before Enabling Night. To do this Families will have to indicate on a sign-up sheet ahead of time that they are planning to attend.

Step 2: Parent Enabling

During this time children will watch a movie or other type of recreation, supervised by older children and teenagers or people who may not be involved in Family Enabling, such as singles and senior citizens.

Sharing Time. Divide parents into small groups of three or four couples each. Couples will share what has been happening in their homes—creative activities, insights, problems, how Family Nights are working, etc. You might want to group couples together who have children of similar ages. (15 minutes)

Enabling Time. Parents meet in large group to receive input and training. In addition to the topic for the evening review the Family Time ideas found in *Family Life Today* (Glendale, Calif.: Gospel Light Publications). Have copies of this magazine available for all families. (25 minutes)

Planning Time. Couples, using input, *Family Life Today,* and other resources, plan activities for their own families on the planning calendar (see chapter 2). Each husband and wife will conclude their time together with a short Scripture portion and prayer. (20 minutes)

Step 3: Family Fellowship

Parents and children meet together to share in a smorgasbord of desserts.

Design Your Own Family Enabling Nights

The concept of a Family Enabling Night is sound—it will work. But feel free to use your own creativity in designing these nights. Don't feel tied to our schedule or to our material. Make your Family Enabling Nights fit the needs of your families. Some churches may want to have such a night once a quarter. Others may prefer a Family Enabling Night once a month. Invite older couples in your church to share in these evenings. Every Family Cluster needs a grandpa and grandma!

Step 2, "Parent Enabling," can be used in many different ways. Basically you have 60 minutes to train parents. Feel free to use lots of variety in your approach to this time. Occasionally, you might want to have guests speak on important family topics. You could have book reviews, listen to tapes, watch films on family topics, or any other type of training you feel is important for parents to receive.

Eleven Family Enabling Nights

The following Family Enabling Night plans are based on chapters from this book. For maximum learning, have parents prepare in advance by reading the chapter on which the Family Enabling Night is based. It would be helpful if each family had a copy of this book.

Family Enabling Session 1

Parents should read chapter 1 before this session.

Step 1: Family Cluster (20 minutes)

Make groups of three to five families each. You may sit them at tables or on the floor. Give each family within the cluster a large sheet of paper (2'x2'), pencils and crayons or magic markers. Explain that each family within the cluster is to draw a picture of their favorite family activity. When the family completes the poster they are to plan a pantomime (silent acting) of their favorite activity. Limit this phase of the family cluster to 15 minutes. During the last 5 minutes of the family cluster, each family has 1 minute to pantomime their activity while the other families within the cluster try to guess what that activity is. When a family finishes their pantomime, they then show their poster to the rest of the group.

Have the cluster group leader close with a word of

prayer and dismiss the children for their hour of activities.

Step 2: Parent Enabling (1 hour)

Sharing (15 minutes). Divide into small groups of three to four couples each. Have parents within the groups share interesting things they have done with their families or things they did in their own families as they were growing up. Limit this to 10 minutes, and then ask groups to share ideas with other groups for 5 minutes.

Enabling (25 minutes). Have parents assemble into a large group for a brainstorming session. Have someone write on a blackboard or overhead projector as parents give as many ideas as possible for family activities. These ideas should be given in rapid-fire succession without explanation or evaluation. Tell people not to take notes—you will give them a chance to copy the ideas later.

After 10 minutes of brainstorming, use 5 minutes for discussion on the activities that have been mentioned. Then allow 5 minutes for parents to copy down the ideas.

Mention the following books as good resources for family activity ideas: Marion Leach Jacobsen, *How to Keep Your Family Together... and Still Have Fun,* Grand Rapids: Zondervan, 1972. Howard G. Hendricks, *Heaven Help the Home!,* (New York: Berkley Publishing Corp., 1975), Gladys Hunt, *Honey for a Child's Heart,* Grand Rapids: Zondervan, 1969.

I suggest you skim through these books and compile a list of activities families can do together. Add to this list local activities, such as parks, museums, and other recreational opportunities, that are available to your families. It would be helpful if you could have this list mimeographed to hand out to parents.

Planning. Give couples a copy of *Family Life Today* and the planning calendar. Explain that they will have 15 minutes to plan family activities. The last 5 minutes, the couples should share in Scripture and prayer together. The Scripture is Deuteronomy 6:4-9. Watch the time and when couples have had 15 minutes of planning, suggest that they move on to the Scripture and prayer time. Single parents may be put into a group where they can share together.

Step 3: Family Fellowship
Families enjoy smorgasbord of desserts together.

Family Enabling Session 2

Step 1: Family Cluster (20 minutes)

Group families in clusters for the "Use-Time-Wisely" activity. You will need: Bibles; about 100 (depending on the size of your group) slips of paper, approximately 2"x3"; a balloon for each cluster; the following list of activities for each cluster:

1. Each family cluster member says "I love you" to five people in other family clusters (group gets total of 5 hours).

2. Keep a balloon in the air for 3 minutes. Each person gets only one hit until all persons in the group have had a hit (total of 4 hours for the group).

3. Each person in the group who memorizes _____ gets 1 hour.

4. Make a human pyramid using everyone in your cluster (10 hours).
5. Sing a special number—LOUD! (6 hours).
6. Entire cluster does jumping jacks together for two minutes (4 hours).
7. Each person must act and sound like a different kind of animal for one minute (group gets total of 7 hours).
8. Each person who plans a good deed to do for someone else this week gets 1 hour.
9. Each person who mentions a blessing gets 1 hour.
10. Whole cluster must smile for 1 minute (group gets a total of 2 hours).

Here's How the Activity Works. Give each family cluster group leader a copy of the above activities. Explain to the groups that they will have 15 minutes to complete as many of the activities as possible. Each group decides which activities they will attempt. Each activity has a number of hours assigned to it. The cluster that successfully completes an activity will receive the number of hours assigned to it. The object of the game is to collect as many hours as possible.

Appoint someone to sit at a table with the slips of paper. When a cluster completes an activity, they are to send their leader to the table to collect the allotted hours. The person making out the slips will write the appropriate number of hours on the slip and give it to the family cluster leader.

This process continues until time is called in 15 minutes. The groups then compute the number of hours they have earned and the cluster with the most time is the winner.

After the winner has been announced, have each family cluster sit together in a circle on the floor. The leader should read Colossians 4, and discuss the following: Why is it important to God that we use our time wisely? Is it important to plan our activities? Why?

Step 2: Parent Enabling (1 hour)

Children are dismissed to movie or other activity.

Sharing (15 minutes). Divide into small groups. Have parents share interesting activities that have been going on in their home. After a few minutes, have groups discuss what they feel is their biggest roadblock to family time.

Enabling. It is important that the leader has read chapter 2 very thoroughly. Explain to the large group that the purpose of this enabling session is to help parents evaluate the quality and quantity of their family time. Explain the Family Time Evaluation Forms 1 and 2 very thoroughly. Give husbands and wives 20 minutes to complete the forms and evaluate their family time. (Single parents can work in a group together.)

Planning. Give parents a copy of *Family Life Today*, a planning calendar (see chap. 2), and any other resources you may have available. Couples should plan for 15 minutes and then conclude with 5 minutes of Scripture and prayer. The Scripture for couples to read is 1 John 4:7-10.

Step 3: Family Fellowship

Families enjoy smorgasbord of desserts together.

Family Enabling Session 3

Step 1: Family Cluster (20 minutes)

Make groups of three to five families each. Each cluster leader should select three families to roleplay the following:

1. You are a family eating dinner in the dining room of your home. Two of the children are misbehaving. One parent corrects the children, but the other parent disagrees with the way things are being handled. Place yourself in this family's situation. Act out the situation the way you feel it happened.

2. You are a family visiting the zoo. In your family no one is in charge and neither parent believes in discipline. Act out how you feel things went at the zoo with this family.

3. You're on a family trip in a car. The children start to

misbehave in the back seat. Mom and Dad, however, believe in discipline and are in agreement on how things should be handled. Act out how you feel this situation was handled.

Give each participating family a chance to plan their roleplay. After each family acts out their role, the group leader should ask the following questions:

What happened in this roleplay? Do you feel there could have been a better way of handling things? How?

Read and briefly discuss Ephesians 6:1-4.

Step 2: Parent Enabling (1 hour)

Sharing (15 minutes). Divide into small groups. Have couples share with one another how their family times have been going. The sharing, however, does not have to be limited to this topic. Parents can share any ideas or concerns they might have.

Enabling and Planning (45 minutes). The purpose of this time will be to help couples start a regular husband-wife together time. Combine your Enabling and Sharing times so you will have 45 minutes for this activity. State that one of the very best ways to develop understanding, communication and spiritual oneness in a marriage is to have a weekly time together. Here's how to get the couples started. Give each couple a mimeographed sheet of paper with the following directions:

1. List five things you feel would be good to discuss together and discuss one of them now.

   (1)

   (2)

   (3)

   (4)

   (5)

108

2. Use the calendar to plan some activities such as Family Night, swimming, etc.
3. Share a Scripture and pray together. Read and discuss Ephesians 5:21-33.
4. Make a list of things you need to pray about together. Pray together remembering to pray for your children and for one another.

Explain each item on the sheet and then have couples sit by themselves to have their together time. Five minutes before the Enabling session is over, have couples come back to a large group. Ask how they feel about what they have just done. After some comments and discussion, suggest that they think about having a regular husband-wife together time.

Step 3: Family Fellowship
Families enjoy a smorgasbord of desserts together.

Family Enabling Session 4

Parents should read chapter 4 before this session.

Step 1: Family Cluster (20 minutes)

Make groups of three to five families each. Give each family within the cluster a large 2'x2' sheet of paper, pencils, crayons, or magic markers, scissors, and glue. Each family should also have several magazines. (You might want parents to bring their own magazines.)

Explain that each family is to make a "What's Important" poster. They may draw, letter, paste on pictures, or decorate their poster in any way they wish. The completed product should show what is important to their family.

Give families 15 minutes to complete this activity. For the final 5 minutes, families within the cluster should explain their posters to one another. Read Matthew 6:19-21. Discuss what these verses have to say about what should be important to us. Have several children close with sentence prayers. Dismiss children for recreation.

Step 2: Parent Enabling (1 hour)

Sharing (15 minutes). Divide into small groups. Have parents share how family times are going, family concerns, interests or any other things they might want to discuss. Another option might be to have them discuss the following question: "What values that you now hold can you attribute directly to your parents' influence?"

Enabling (25 minutes). Read chapter 4 thoroughly before this session. Ask the group for definitions of "values." Values are the things we feel are important. Ask for examples of specific Christian values. When we arrange values in order of priority, we have a value system.

Prepare copies of the values list in chapter 4 for each couple. Explain that you are going to give each couple a sheet with a list of values which they are to rank in the order of importance. Next, parents should find an appropriate Scripture to go with each value (have several concordances or topical Bibles available).

After values have been ranked, have couples ask themselves the following questions about each value:

What am I presently doing to teach these values to my children?

What can I do to teach these values?

Planning (20 minutes). Give each couple or parent a copy of *Family Life Today,* a planning calendar, and any other Family Time resources you might have. Couples should plan for 15 minutes and then conclude with 5 minutes of Scripture and prayer. The Scripture for couples to read is Psalm 78:1-8.

Step 3: Family Fellowship

Families enjoy a smorgasbord of desserts together.

Family Enabling Session 5

Parents should read chapter 5 before this session.

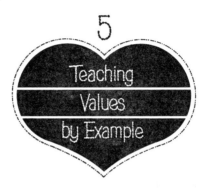

Step 1: Family Cluster (20 minutes)

Make small groups of families. Have the leader of each family cluster start the following three games. Each game is to last 5 minutes only.

1. Simon Says. Select someone to be the game leader. When the game leader says "Simon Says" the rest of the group must do what Simon says. However if the game leader asks the group to do something without saying "Simon Says" first, no one is to do it. If someone follows his command, they are the next to be "Simon."

2. Who's the Leader? One person is chosen to be "it" and is sent from the room. Another person is chosen to be the leader. The group must imitate whatever the leader does. For example, if the leader scratches

his nose the rest of the group must do the same. However, the object of the game is to try to keep "it" from discovering who the leader is. Call "it" back into the room and explain that he is to try to discover the leader. If the "leader" is discovered by "it," the leader becomes "it" and leaves the room while the group selects a new leader. Play this game for five minutes.

3. Follow the Leader. Everyone gets into the act in this game. Choose a leader. The rest of the group must follow his actions for one minute. At the end of the minute, that leader can appoint another person to be the leader. Follow this process for 5 minutes.

Read John 13:14,15 and 1 Peter 5:3 to your cluster and discuss the following:

(1) Name two people, living or dead, who you feel are good examples to follow.

(2) In what ways can we be good examples for others to follow?

Close in prayer and dismiss the children for recreation.

Step 2: Parent Enabling (1 hour)

Sharing (15 minutes). Divide into small groups. Have persons share how their family times are going, family concerns, interests, or any other items they might want to discuss. Another option is to have groups discuss the following question: "What specific actions or attitudes do you see in your children's lives that indicate they are following your example?"

Enabling, Large Group (25 minutes). Ask if some of the parents would share the personal examples they talked about in their small groups.

Summarize the identification process and Scriptures

on teaching by example given on pages 38–40.

Discuss. What are some reasons that a "much-loved child" is more apt to follow the example of his parents? What are some practical ways to show a child that he is "much-loved?"

Prepare a copy of the following "Teach By Example" sheet for each person.

Explain how to use the "Teach by Example" sheet and allow parents to spend the remainder of the Enabling Time filling out the sheet.

Planning (20 minutes). Give parents a copy of *Family Life Today,* a planning calendar and any other resources you may have available. Couples should plan for 15 minutes and then conclude with 5 minutes of Scripture and prayer. The Scripture for couples to read and discuss is Ephesians 5:1,2.

Step 3: Family Fellowship
Families enjoy smorgasbord of desserts together.

Teach by Example
DEMONSTRATE!

1. Decide
What value would you like to demonstrate?

_____

2. Develop
What does God's Word have to say about that value?

_____

_____

_____

What changes do I need to make in my own life?

_____

_____

_____

3. Demonstrate
List at least three ways you will demonstrate this value
to your children.

_____

_____

_____

Family Enabling Session 6

Step 1: Family Cluster (20 minutes)

Make groups of three to five families each. Seat people in a circle on the floor. Give each person a small slip of paper and a pencil. Explain that each person is to write down a question he feels would be interesting to discuss. These questions should be about the Bible or the Christian life. Questions such as "What is your favorite Bible verse?" and "What do you think heaven will be like?" are appropriate.

Give families about 5 minutes to complete their questions and then have them fold the sheets and place them in a bowl in the middle of the circle. Next, have a child draw a slip and read it to the cluster. Discuss the question for a few minutes and then draw another question. Continue this process until Family Cluster time is up.

Step 2: Parent Enabling (1 hour)

Sharing (15 minutes). Divide into small groups of three or four couples each. Have persons share how their family times are going, family concerns, interests, or any other things they might want to discuss.

Enabling (25 minutes). A good way to help people visualize the potential of Family Nights with their own family is to show them pictures of other families having Family Nights. Try to have slides taken of families having Family Nights. Show the slides at this time.

Ask several couples who have Family Nights to give a brief testimony of what Family Nights have done for their families. Have these same parents answer questions from the rest of the group on the "how-to" of Family Nights.

Next, ask others to share interesting things they have done for Family Nights.

Give *Family Life Today* to each couple and review all four Family Time plans. Give an example of how you would use that plan with your own family.

Planning (20 minutes). Give couples a planning calendar and 15 minutes to specifically plan Family Nights for the next month. The final 5 minutes of this time is for couples to have Scripture and prayer together. The Scripture for the couples to read is Psalm 127.

Step 3: Family Fellowship

Families enjoy smorgasbord of desserts together. On this night, we suggest you ask parents to bring desserts that the children especially enjoy.

Family Enabling Session 7

Parents should read chapter 7 before this session.

7

Creating Family
Unity at the
Dinner Hour

Step 1: Family Cluster (20 minutes)

For the start of this cluster, individual families should be alone, preferably at a card table. Give families the following instructions:

Children are to vote secretly on one word to give to Dad and one word to give to Mother. Words like hurt, funny, kiss, vacation, afraid, and surprise work quite well. When children decide what word to give their parents, they should say the parent's name, and the word, for example "Dad-hurt." Then Dad must respond with a story from his childhood based on the word "hurt." Then Mom is to be given a word.

Give families 5 minutes to complete this activity.

Then have each cluster of families sit on the floor in large circles. Each child in the cluster is to think of one new thing he learned about his parents and tell the rest of the group.

Have someone read Proverbs 15:17. Discuss. Is this verse true? Why?

Now go around the cluster with each person finishing the sentence "Better mealtimes happen when _____."

If you have any extra time, have the group decide on five rules to make mealtimes happy times.

Step 2: Parent Enabling (1 hour)

Sharing (15 minutes). Divide into small groups of three to four couples each. Have persons share how their family times are going, family concerns, interests, or any other things they might want to discuss. Another option is to ask groups to discuss the following two questions: "What are your memories of mealtimes in your family when you were growing up?"; "Are there things you would like to change with your own family?"

Enabling (25 minutes). As a large group, think of all the problems that sometimes happen at mealtimes. Have someone list these on a blackboard as they are given. Next, form groups of six people each and assign several of the problems to each group. Give groups 10 minutes to design creative solutions to the problems. Have groups share their solutions with the large group.

For the remaining time, have a "Delightful Dinner Time" brainbust. Have parents think of as many good ideas as possible to make dinner time a delight. Ideas can be topics of conversations, good menus, games, centerpieces, read-aloud material or any other helpful suggestions.

Planning (20 minutes). Give each parent or couple a

copy of *Family Life Today,* a planning calendar, and any other family time resources you might have available. Couples should plan for 15 minutes and then conclude with 5 minutes of Scripture and prayer. Suggest that parents plan some creative things to do at the dinner table.

The Scripture for couples to read is Galatians 5:22-26.

Step 3: Family Fellowship

Families enjoy a smorgasbord of desserts together.

Family Enabling Session 8

Parents should read chapter 8 before this session.

Step 1: Family Cluster (20 minutes)

Make groups of three to five families each. Give each family within the cluster paper and pencils. Explain that each family is to prepare for a Family Cluster Bible study. The Scripture to study is Ephesians 4:31,32. Give families 10 minutes to choose and do two of the suggested activities on page 70. Form your clusters again and have each family share the results of their activities.

Close your Bible study with a sentence prayer from one person in each family.

Step 2: Parent Enabling (1 hour)

Sharing (15 minutes). Divide into small groups of three to four couples each. Have persons share how their family times are going, family concerns, interests, or any other things they might want to discuss.

Enabling (25 minutes). Prepare a "Family Bible Study Prepare and Share Worksheet" for each person. Group parents into "families" of five or six persons each. Explain that each group is a family and will have a family Bible study on Matthew 6:24-34. The "family" is to decide together which two activities they will do to prepare for the family Bible study. Each person within the family should read the Scripture and do the two activities. Give persons 10 minutes to prepare the activities and then 10 minutes to share with one another within their "families" the content of their two activities and any insights they gained from the study.

Planning (20 minutes). Give each parent or couple a copy of *Family Life Today,* a planning calendar and any other family time resources you might have. Couples should plan for 15 minutes and then conclude with 5 minutes of Scripture and prayer. The Scripture for couples to read is Colossians 3:12-17.

Step 3: Family Fellowship
Families enjoy a smorgasbord of desserts together.

Family Enabling Session 9

Step 1: Family Cluster (20 minutes)

Make groups of three to five families each. Give the head of each family a list of the Scriptures to memorize (last page of chapter 9). Each family should also have several magazines and scissors. Explain that each family is to select one verse to memorize as a family. Families should: (1) Talk about why the Scripture is important to memorize; (2) Have a good understanding of what the Scripture means; (3) Cut a picture out of a magazine that reminds them of the Scripture; (4) Memorize the Scripture together as a family.

Give families 15 minutes for this project. Then have each family share what they discussed with the rest of the family cluster.

Step 2: Parent Enabling (1 hour)

Sharing (15 minutes). Divide into small groups of three or four couples each. Have persons share how their family times are going, family concerns, interests, or any other things they might want to discuss. Another option is to have groups discuss how knowing certain Scripture verses, or Scripture portions, has helped them in their Christian walk.

Enabling (25 minutes). Go step by step through the "RULE" of family Scripture memorization given in chapter 9.

Have parents look at the section entitled "Memorizing Scripture on Family Night" in chapter 9. Suggest that families accept the challenge to memorize one Scripture a month together as a family and start the project with a special Family Night.

Explain the Card Game on pages 78, 79. Give each couple or parent a stack of 3x5 index cards. Have parents take the first three verses divided into phrases and print those phrases on the index cards. When this project is complete, if time allows, you might divide into groups of five or six and have parents play the game.

Planning (20 minutes). Give each couple or parent a copy of *Family Life Today*, a planning calendar and any other family time resources you might have. Suggest that parents plan when they will do their family memory project. Couples should plan for 15 minutes and then conclude with 5 minutes of Scripture and prayer. The Scripture for couples to read is Psalm 1.

Step 3: Family Fellowship

Families enjoy a smorgasbord of desserts together.

Family Enabling Session 10

Parents should read chapter 10 before this session.

Step 1: Family Cluster (20 minutes)

Make family clusters of three to five families each. Then each family should, in their own family circle, discuss the following two questions: "What has God done for our family?" and "What has God taught us through various circumstances?" The family should assign one member to be ready to share this with the rest of the cluster. Each family should also look in the book of Proverbs for a Scripture that speaks of God teaching us.

Each family should then share the two questions they discussed with the rest of the family cluster and read the passage they chose from Proverbs.

Step 2: Parent Enabling (1 hour)

Sharing (15 minutes). Read chapter 10 thoroughly

before this session. Make notes on the things you feel are important to share with the group. Read Deuteronomy 6:4-9, especially noting verses 7-9. Ask for comments from the group on what implications these verses have for twentieth-century Christians.

Next, have parents count off in groups of not more than six. Give each person a few minutes to answer the following questions individually:

1. What opportunities have I used to teach my children informally during the past month?
2. What opportunity to teach my children informally did I miss?
3. When did God teach me a lesson in an informal way?

Give groups 15 minutes to discuss these questions and then ask if any person would like to share something specific from any one of the three questions they answered. Allow several people to share.

Planning (20 minutes). Give each couple or parent a copy of *Family Life Today,* a planning calendar and any other family time resources you might have. Couples should plan for 15 minutes and then conclude with 5 minutes of Scripture and prayer. The Scripture for couples to read is Hebrews 12:2-11.

Step 3: Family Fellowship

Families enjoy a smorgasbord of desserts together.

Family Enabling Session 11

Parents should read chapter 11 before this session.

Step 1: Family Cluster (20 minutes)

This activity will need advance planning. Ask families to come prepared to share pictures of a family vacation or outing. Slides work well, but if families do not have slides, they could bring pictures to show or set up a small display of souvenirs, maps, etc., of their trip.

Give each family a chance to show their pictures and tell about the trip. You will probably want to give families a specific amount of time for their presentations. Other families may get good ideas for future vacations and other recreational activities. This session will work especially well a couple of months before summer vacations. (This may take more than the allotted family cluster time. If so, adjust your other activities to compensate for this extra amount of time.)

Step 2: Parent Enabling (1 hour)

Sharing (15 minutes). Divide into small groups of three or four couples each. Have persons share how their family times are going, family concerns, interests, or other things they might want to discuss.

Enabling (25 minutes). This activity too will take some advance preparation. Tell parents well in advance that they are to come prepared to share one good recreational idea with the rest of the group. This could be a craft, place to go, game, etc. Parents should give as much detail as possible about the recreational activity. Suggest that if some parents cannot think of a recreational idea they would like to share that they could go to the local library and find something suitable.

Planning (20 minutes). Give each couple or parent a copy of *Family Life Today*, a planning calendar and any other family time resources you might have. Couples should plan for 15 minutes and then conclude with 5 minutes of Scripture and prayer. The Scripture for couples to read is Matthew 5:13-16.

Step 3: Family Fellowship

Families enjoy a smorgasbord of desserts together.